"Searc

The Trans...

Introduction

On Thursday evening, May 26, 1966 the gymnasium at Newton Community High School was very crowded and very warm. The 176 members of the graduating Class of 1966 were making their way from the cafeteria down the hallway, around the corner and midway down the hallway behind the gym to enter through the back door two by two. The boys were wearing the standard royal blue caps and gowns and the girls in their standard white.

The parents, grandparents, aunts, uncles, brothers, sisters, cousins and anyone else that could be coaxed into coming, were ready for the ceremony to begin. The graduates were especially ready for a number of reasons. First, it was very hot and uncomfortable in the aforementioned caps and gowns. Second, we really didn't care that much about the speeches from invited guests and the valedictorian etc. We just wanted to get the diploma, and get out of the caps and gowns.

And third, and probably most important to many of the graduates, we were ready to get to the graduation party on the bluff above Love's ford.

Yes.....we were going to the graduation party to congratulate ourselves on completing the four year requirement of high school, and to once again prove that we could drink large quantities of cheap beer and tell stories about our life experiences, some of which were even true. That night the realities of life after graduation were not permitted to enter your mind. This was a night for celebration and raucous behavior. No thoughts of college and higher education on this night, no thoughts of jobs or possible military service, or responsibilities.

But, nights end and daylight comes. And the next morning when the sun came up, the simple reality that I had to get home and go to work at the Fairview Drive-In did indeed creep into my aching head. The short lived celebration was over. And in the real world another day had begun. Although the Class of 1966 didn't want to be thrust headlong into the real world just yet, with the signing of our diplomas by Emory Gifford, Principal and two members of the Board of Education of district 127, we were allowed to go out in to the world and fend for ourselves.

In all honesty, some members of our class knew exactly what they wanted to do. Many had already made plans for college, some had decided on a major and a minor. Many were taking advantage of their academic scholarships. Some were heading off to college, but didn't really know how they would pay for it. Their parents certainly didn't have the money to pay for a college education. But at least they had a direction. They knew what they wanted to do, and were ready to get started.

Unfortunately though, many of us didn't have a clue what direction to go. I include myself in that sizable group. My parents wanted me to go to college to get some form of higher education, but I and many like me didn't have any idea what we wanted to do or be. High school had been a lot of fun. But fun didn't equal doing well in school. My "guidance counselor," after looking at my grades and class position percentile, suggested maybe I should look at a vocational school. It was sort of like an old movie, where two convicts had finally figured out a way to escape from prison, and once they were out on the street, they didn't have a clue what to do or which direction to go. I know that's the way I felt, and I believe I can safely say that a lot of my male classmates felt the same way.

Meanwhile, 6800 miles away in Viet Nam, things were taking a new direction. By the end of 1966 the U. S. military had committed 385,300 troops to the war[1]. Thoughts of the future by young men and women, their parents, their friends, or future employers couldn't help but be affected by the brutal news of the war that came into homes across America via the evening news and in newspapers on a daily basis. Try as we might to ignore it, it was real and it wasn't going away anytime soon.

This is not a book about the Viet Nam war, in the sense of whose strategy was best, or what politicians were responsible for messing things up the worst. History is replete with theories and blunders and mistakes that were made during the Viet Nam war, and how the U.S. could have won the war but for some of those blunders and mistakes. No....this book is about how the lives of many of my classmates, friends, relatives, and their families were directly affected by the changes in time and culture, war and politics. It was a time of dealing with tumult, consternation, race, radicalism in many forms, and still maintaining the strong family traditions and values that made growing up in the mid-west, in a small community, with our family and friends close by, an enviable place to be.

This book will go beyond "The Innocent Age"(my first book) in many ways. Mainly it will document the changes that took place in my life, and the lives of many of my relatives and friends because of a war, the search for a direction in life, and how we dealt with the realities of life that came from that. Most all of the people that will be mentioned in this writing have given permission for various events in their lives to be discussed. Some names will be in "quotation marks" indicating that a name has been changed. That simply means that I did not receive permission from that person or never had the opportunity to speak with them about the book. It won't affect the facts or the meaning of any of the stories.

When the members of the "Greatest Generation" came home after World War II, they literally began producing the "Baby Boomer" generation. I have no doubt that they hoped with all their heart and soul that their efforts in that war would mean that their sons and daughters would never have to go through anything like that. But as happens from generation to generation, the "Baby Boomers" now had their battles to fight. Some in the hot, steamy, wet, muddy, snake infested jungles of Viet Nam and some right here in the U.S.A. They searched for a direction, searched for a reason, searched for the right person, searched for the answers.

They were searching for everything. They were making a transition, and sometimes the reality they found was cruel.

Part One

The Darkening Clouds

The summer of 1966 was not that much different than any other summer, other than the fact that I was now considered to be a young adult, with a high school diploma. I was happy to be out of high school, as were most of my friends. The problem was, I had the feeling of drifting down stream in a canoe and I had forgotten to bring any paddles. I was of course helping my parents at the Fairview Drive-In Theater. Business was strong, and the list of movies for that year was the reason why. Admittedly there weren't a lot of other places to go for entertainment at the time, but people wanted to see these films.

"The Good, the Bad, and the Ugly" with Clint Eastwood-Eli Wallach-Lee Van Cleef. "Stagecoach" with Ann Margret- Alex Cord- Red Buttons- Mike Connors. "One Million Years B.C." with Raquel Welch....yeah Raquel Welch, need I say more. The promotional pictures of that movie, with Raquel wearing what was supposedly the latest fashion for women of that era, got the attention of many young men, me included. The movie itself was just so-so, but Raquel in that little furry outfit...well ok, you get the point.

The fact is that most eighteen year old young men were much more interested in cars, good looking ladies, music and being able to get some beer for the weekend, than we were in our jobs, our first semester of college, or the war in Viet Nam. The war however, was like a ringing in your ears. You ignored it for the most part. You went on with your life, but it was there, buzzing in the background and it wouldn't go away.

My cousin Roger went to work at the local Marathon station that summer, the one formerly owned by my dad. It was now operated by a very sturdily built man by the name of Dick Tracy. Yes that was his real name. Dick had coal black hair, and a no BS look about him, but he was indeed one of the nicest, fairest men that you could ever meet.

Across the street from the Marathon station was Tony Hunt's barber shop. Tony had become a close friend of both Roger and me. I don't remember how we first met Tony, however he was a 1963 graduate of N.C.H.S. When we had time off from our jobs, we would hang out in the barber shop and gamble in some form. We would either slide quarters, to see who could get closest to the wall, or bounce quarters in a cup. Occasionally a quick poker game, in between customers, would break out. The gambling debts could go as high as $10.00, and on occasion maybe even up to $15.00 to $20.00 depending on how many hours we got to stay in the barber shop. Now ten to twenty dollars might not sound like much money today, but at the time if you cleared $60.00 or $70.00 a week from your job, that was pretty good money. I know at the time I was making $50.00 a week working for my dad, which of course included getting to live at home.

With Tony being about three years older than me, and a couple years older than Roger, it meant that he could legally buy beer. Well, Roger and I took advantage of that fact on many occasions. It was a fact that the hobbies and interest of young boys changed as they got into their teen years and older. So having a fast car, a good looking girlfriend or date, and a cooler full of cheap beer was about all a directionless high school graduate from Newton, IL could ask for.

That particular summer, after graduation, there were many occasions when we would not go 24 hours without having a cooler full of Schlitz beer. If there wasn't a party somewhere, we would simply go out in the country somewhere with the cooler, a guitar and harmonica, and make our own party. So, at least for those few hours of fun, we were not thinking about the fact that we didn't have a plan for the future, or that we would more than likely, at some point have to go to war. But many times there were parties. Most times it was "bring your own", but sometimes it was a "kegger," and you pitched in a five dollar bill, and you could drink as much as you want. Think about it. You could buy a six pack of cheap beer of some kind for $1.25, $1.50 tops. So if you could drink $5.00 worth in someone's basement, man that was cool. The first time I was with "Lori" was at one such party.

I had met "Lori" after a football game during my junior year in high school. She was sitting with "Ruby" in the bleachers. Apparently there must have been a "sock hop" after the football game. That night though, I was more interested in "Ruby". And she was kind enough to bring up the fact that I had made a couple of tackles in the game that night, and one thing led to another, and "Ruby and "Lori" allowed me and my cousin Jerry Woods to take them home from the dance. What a bit of good luck that was. We went to "Ruby's" house eventually, and just parked right there in the driveway. Cousin Jerry in the back seat with "Lori" and me in the front with "Ruby." We stayed there for a long time, before we eventually had to get "Lori" either to her car or to her house. Now I know this all seems harmless enough, and it was for the most part. The only problem was that Jerry and I were supposed to be in Vincennes, IN by 8:30 the next morning to take the obligatory SAT test.

Personally, I could not have cared less about that test. I really didn't have any clue as to what I wanted to do. But my parents were determined that I should get a college degree in something. So I got home around 12:30 and probably was supposed to meet up with Jerry around 7:00 am the next morning, and head out to Vincennes. We finally found the school and the correct auditorium, found the coffee machine, and went in for the test. Aside from being really tired, and really sleepy, I didn't understand a lot of the problems in front of me, thus I did very poorly on the test, and thus the recommendation from the "guidance counselor" that I enroll in a vocational school somewhere.

The meeting of both "Lori" and "Ruby" would however become a much bigger part of my life in the coming years. More about that a little later.

In the meantime, that little ringing in your ears that wouldn't go away, called Viet Nam was getting louder. Thousands and thousands of troops were being trained as quickly as possible to be ready to deploy. Many young men knew that it was just a matter of time until they would be drafted. If you didn't have a legitimate college exemption or didn't already have a family, more than likely you were going to be called up. Roger was already 18 and registered with the draft board. As soon as I turned 18 on July 30th of that summer, I also registered as was required. But Roger, with no real direction in to the future, had already been talking to his good friend Eddie Groves about the possibility of joining the Marine Corps. They both knew it was a certainty that eventually they would be drafted.

To this day there is still a controversy about who had the brilliant idea to go and talk to the Marine Corps recruiter that summer, probably in August of 1966. Roger claims that Eddie called and said that if they would go in to Wagy's café and talk to the Marine recruiter, he would buy them lunch. Eddie apparently believes that it was Roger's idea to meet with the guy, but the controversy aside, the fact is that they did indeed meet the Marine recruiter that day, he did buy them lunch, and after talking to them through lunch told them "well boys, I just don't know. You know we only take the best, and quite frankly I just don't think you guys are up to Marine Corps standards."

So, Roger at least was offended that the recruiter would say that. So he says "Wait a minute, what do you mean we're not Marine Corps material, we most certainly are." Roger had spent the last three years playing football for Frank Chizevsky, and thought, I suppose, how much worse could it be. Eddie was just plain big, strong and not to be messed with, even though he had a big smile on his face most of the time. So after some "reconsideration" from the recruiter he allowed them to enlist in the Marine Corps.

They went in on the buddy plan, and decided that they could leave in late December. They would also be together in boot camp. Other than that there were no special deals. So now it got even more intense. Roger went home from Wagy's café and told his parents that he had enlisted in the Marine Corps, and although Roger can't remember the exact language, his dad, my Uncle Wayne, called him an idiot for doing that in the middle of the Viet Nam war.

If there was one thing that helped bring some light into what seemed to be a rather dark time, it was the music of the 60's, especially from the mid 1960's on into the early 70's.

The Beatles were still the kings. They were turning out albums one after another, including "Hard Days Night" in 1964, "Rubber Soul" in 1965, "Help" in 1966, then "Revolver" in 1966, then in the summer of 1967, "Sgt. Pepper's Lonely Hearts Club Band" only to be followed in late 1967 with "Magical Mystery Tour". And there was much more to come a little later. Also in the mix were The Rolling Stones, The Doors, Jimi Hendrix, Buffalo Springfield, The Beach Boys, Cream, and so many more.

There were also several Chicago based bands that were very popular in the area. The Cryan' Shames, The Shadows of Knight, The New Colony Six, and the Buckingham's all got a ton of airplay and local bands covered them a lot. It's easy to see why guys with no real direction became so infatuated with the music scene from that era. I know that I and many of my friends couldn't wait to get some guys together and start playing that music ourselves, in front of people that also loved it. There will be a lot more about bands and playing music a little later.

So, as the summer of 1966 continued and slowly turned into Fall, the intensity and frequency of partying continued as well. I guess that Roger and I, along with many of our classmates and friends thought if we could just keep laughing and having fun, and drinking enough beer that any bad thoughts or circumstances would be held at bay.

Whether you were a young man or young woman, the threat of having to become a responsible adult and follow the rules just seemed to be asking a little too much. Generation after generation has had to deal with those feelings, but at the time, it was as though we were the only ones. As selfish as it was, I believe that was the general attitude of the time.

Roger sold his old red and white 1956 Pontiac and purchased a yellow 1964 Dodge Dart GT. It had a little 273 cubic inch V8 engine, 4-speed with a Hurst shifter, mag wheels, and bucket seats, man it was sharp, and surprisingly fast for such a small V8. Tony Hunt had a navy blue 1965 Mustang fastback 2+2, 289 V8, factory 4-speed. It was also a very sharp car, and also surprisingly fast for a small V8. I think you can probably see this scenario coming. Roger and Tony were constantly challenging each other to drag races. And 99% of the time it would take place on the Bogota blacktop. They would race all the way down to the area that had been marked off as the “unofficial Bogota dragstrip”, race a few times there, and generally race most of the way back toward Route 33. Most of the time it would turn out about 50-50 wins for both of them. That was the frustrating part of it, and why it went on day after day, time after time. But it was certainly fun to watch. It got so bad, that from time to time, Tony would actually close the barber shop just to go race Roger for bragging rights. And so it went, back and forth, on and on.

The old Bogota black top, and the “unofficial Bogota dragstrip” was known far and wide by guys that thought they had a pretty hot car, and wanted to prove it to whoever would take their challenge.

Sometimes on a Saturday or Sunday afternoon there would be so many cars down there it became known as “the Bogota Nationals”, a takeoff on the actual U. S. Nationals drag races in Indianapolis. I was there many times with my black and white 58 Pontiac, and fortunately came away victorious on many occasions. Sometimes the neighbors at the end of the “strip” would bring lawn chairs out and sit in the yard by the road and watch us. They didn’t seem to mind that we usually turned around in their driveway. Even then we knew that it was somewhat dangerous to be racing there, but to my knowledge, no one ever wrecked their car there and no one was injured, so I suppose we were just lucky. But as I stated earlier, young men have different hobbies and interest after the teen years arrive. Cars, women, partying, music.....right or wrong that's the way it was, and most of us lived to tell stories about it.

I was working for my dad at the Fairview Drive-In that summer, helping with the mowing, painting, small construction projects and so forth, but I wasn't working at the box office regularly or running the projectors. I would learn that skill a little later. I was earning $50.00 a week, which at the time was enough to pay for gas for my old reliable '58 Pontiac, food at the Dog and Suds, my share of the beer, and make the payment on the note at the bank for my car. I don't remember the exact monthly amount on the note, but it was my responsibility.

My dad was adamant that I pay for my own car. He went with me to speak with Mr. Pickerel, then the president of the Peoples State Bank, when it came time to buy the Pontiac, but he assured Mr. Pickerel that I would be making the payments on the note. That was all about the process of learning the value of a dollar, and about taking better care of something, if you owned it. It was also about learning to save part of your earnings instead of blowing it all on just having a good time.

So, here's what all that is leading up to. On Sunday August 21, 1966 the Beatles were coming to Busch Memorial Stadium in St. Louis to perform one show. My cousin Steve Kinder from Centralia called me on or around August 15th with some really exciting news.

He said that he had talked to a guy that had four tickets to the concert, but that he wasn't going to be able to go, and offered them to Steve for $12.00 apiece, and he had one for me. I was a totally committed fan of the Beatles. I had every album, every single, couldn't get enough information about them etc. etc., but $12.00. Man, $12.00 was almost a quarter of my entire paycheck for the week. So I told Steve, "Hey I'll have to give that some thought, and I'll call you back." Steve says, "What do you mean you'll have to call me back. We're talking about tickets to go see the Beatles here man, what is there to think about?" He was right of course. It should have been a no brainer. But at the time I was going over the numbers in my head and figured that if the ticket was $12.00 and there would be gas, food, maybe some beer, plus if I had to drive in to St. Louis, I had never done that before. And so I stalled. I said "Man I hate to turn this down, but I just don't think I can afford to do it." "I'm only making $50.00 bucks a week."

Well Steve was in total disbelief that I was turning down a chance to go see the greatest band to come along in our lifetime because the ticket cost $12.00. And I certainly did take a lot of ridiculing and well placed insults from anyone that I told about it, but at the time it seemed like the right thing to do.

So the Beatles played to about 23,000 screaming fans on that Sunday, in a heavy rain. The show was not a sellout. Some were hesitant to come because of the heavy rain, fearing the show would be cancelled. The Beatles had played a gig in Cincinnati earlier that day, starting at 12:00 noon, and immediately got on the plane to head for St. Louis. It was on the way from Cincinnati to St. Louis that the Beatles decided to a man to stop touring[2]. Afterwards I also found out that the actual ticket price was $5.50, so the guy who sold cousin Steve four tickets at $12.00 apiece made a nice profit. That only eased the pain of not seeing the Beatles live for a little while. I've actually regretted it my entire life. But, you do what you think is right at the time, and move on.

Part Two

Rumbling in the Distance

Just like the little jolt that you get from static electricity, when you touch the door knob after you walk across a carpet, or someone scoots their feet on the floor and touches your ear and that little spark makes you jump and move away... that was the feeling I got when the news of the carnage going on in Viet Nam came in to the living room on the TV every evening.

Make no mistake, I was in support of the U.S. policy to defeat the North Vietnamese and the Viet Cong. I supported every single soldier and Marine on the ground there, and hoped that they could do their jobs swiftly and come home. If the Air Force and Navy could shell and bomb enough places, and the NVA and Viet Cong gave up, I was all for it.

But as my generation watched the U.S. troop count climb and the casualties on all sides go up daily, the need for some way to take our thoughts in a different direction intensified. Certainly dating was one way. "Lori" and I had been dating since my senior year and that continued to go fairly well.

But music and "washing" away the thoughts of war were really the favorite pastime for me, and I think I can safely say, many of my friends. During the summer and fall of 1966 the music scene in Newton was actually pretty good. The Nite Raiders was a relatively new band, made up of a few of my classmates, and a young kid from the Chicago area. They were practicing and improving and rolling along pretty well. The Trifaris from Effingham would also come over and play at the teen center, known as "The Spot." "The Spot's" first location was on the corner of S. Van Buren and E. Washington St., across the road from Douthit Drugs. It was named "the Spot" because there was a sign painted on the north side of the building. My memory tells me that it was a paint sign that had a bullseye on it, thus "The Spot".

My cousin Steve was part of a band from Centralia called The Epics. Steve was the lead guitarist. The Epics would come through Newton from time to time when they were playing in Oblong or Olney at the teen centers there. Steve and his brother Rick would usually stay with me or Roger and sometimes at the Massey's house. The Massey's were friends of Steve's family from back in the days when my uncle Dick was playing music in the late

40’s and early 50’s. He too was an excellent guitar player.

One summer night after the Epics had finished playing a job at the “Teen Tower” in Oblong, Steve’s 1957 Chevy was headed back toward Newton looking for someplace to return a case of “Little Joe” bottles for credit toward another case. In the car was cousin Rick, their friend from Centralia, Steve Schwartz, my good friend Mike Yager-Kenny’s little brother- and me. We ended up at the Black Top in Dietrich. We had finished the remaining beers on the way.

So Steve grabs the empty case of bottles and heads in to the bar. Steve was not yet 21 years old, but he could get served almost anywhere. His hairline had been receding since he was about 15, so he looked older plus he was very, shall we say confident in himself, and had a very deep voice to go along with it, so he very seldom even got carded. So with a new case of the seven ounce beers, we headed back toward Newton, listening to the radio, drinking the “Little Joe’s” and spinning tales about all types of adventures.

We were about a mile west of “Beams Corner” going about 70 miles an hour, when for no apparent reason, Steve Schwartz, sitting in the middle of the front seat, grabs the steering wheel and gives it a hard jerk to the right and starts laughing like crazy. The car swerved sharply to the right, then sharply back to the left. We were all grabbing whatever we could to keep from being thrown around the car. Steve managed to straighten the car up a little just before we entered the ditch, fortunately going straight down the ditch instead of through it.

The ditch was full of water, and immediately the water came gushing up through the boot of the shifter, which had been converted to a three speed on the floor from the column. So water is flying all through the car—Steve is trying to see where he's going, all the while trying to guide the car out of the ditch and back on the road. Schwartz is no longer laughing; he's hanging on for dear life along with the rest of us.

We got back on the highway about a half mile west of "Beams Corner" and the cussing and threatening of Schwartz began. We were all angry, yet glad to be alive. My cousins Steve and Rick were really angry. They were already pounding on Schwartz while we were still going down the highway. We turned north at "Beams Corner" and continued up until we found a road to pull onto going east. At that point everyone was bailing out of the car, and Schwartz took off down the road with Steve in hot pursuit. I certainly was expecting Steve to beat him within an inch of his life, but mostly it was a lot of hollering and cussing and asking him what in the hell he was thinking. Eventually everyone calmed down, talked about how lucky we were, and had another beer.

That night happened to be one of the nights that Steve was staying at the Massey home. I have no idea what time we all arrived there, but I made the call home and told my dad that I was staying in town with the rest of the crew. I remember that we raided the refrigerator and fixed eggs and bacon and whatever else we could find and all went up to find a bed to crash in. The next morning, Steve rousted everyone out of bed before any of us were really ready to get up, but they had to get back to Centralia.

The car was still wet inside the next morning, but we all decided it would be fun to go see where we went in the ditch and so forth. When we found the tracks that led into the ditch on the west end of the "accident", we all saw at the same time that about 20 yards after we entered the ditch, we had missed a power pole by about a foot.

The tracks continued on for about another fifty yards to where we exited the ditch. It got rather quiet in the car for a little while, as we were all considering the "what could have been" in that situation. Everyone realized that we were very lucky to have been just wet and scared. Schwartz apologized to everyone, and that was the end of it. Fortunately we all lived to talk about it, and we certainly did that for years to come.

So even though I didn't really want to go to college just yet, I did enroll at Olney Community College, now called Olney Central College. OCC was founded in 1963, and sat on what had been the grounds and offices of the Pure Oil Company. The student union building was just to the northwest of the main building, and had apparently been a cafeteria/break area for employees of the company. There were some tables to play cards, a TV room, and plenty of room to just hang out.

I guess the biggest surprise for me in attending college was to find out that your instructors didn't really care if you attended class or not. If you were there for the first few classes, you knew the assignments, you took the mid-term and final exams, it was all good.

I remember an American History instructor, Mr. Horan, that said on the first day of class, "I don't really care if you attend my class or not. I don't care if you come in here and eat lunch as long as you don't bother your neighbor. My tests will be straight out of the book. Conversations about current events that may go on in class will have no bearing on either the mid-term or the final exam." So I thought well hell, this isn't so bad. He doesn't care if I'm here, and I certainly don't care if I'm here, so this should work just fine. I remember one day when he was playing cards in the union building with us, when he got up to go to class, and I just said "ok see you later."

I stayed there and continued to play cards. Not all the instructors were that laid back about it though. Some expected you to show up, pay attention and participate. Frankly, I just wasn't into it. I was much more interested in girls, cars, beer and music.

My friend and classmate Ron Stephenson and I shared driving back and forth to Olney at least for a while that fall and maybe on into the next year as well. Ron was a much more serious student than I was. I think he had already figured out that he wanted to be either in radio or possibly some type of sports writer.

I also remember that we both signed up for a wrestling class one semester. It was actually a P.E. class, but the instructor Mr. Salmon, had been on a wrestling team in college somewhere, and was really serious about it. When the class started, and we had learned enough of the basics to actually start wrestling, the instructor paired Ron and I together to start what was actually like a round robin competition. The winner would go on to meet the winner of the next match etc.

Well, Ron Stephenson outweighed me by about 40 pounds. I was a skinny punk kid, but I was pretty fast, and weighed probably about 155 pounds. Ron was quite husky and weighed about 200 pounds at the time, so even though I might be successful in getting the first move on him, he could muscle his way around and once he got on top, I was done. I couldn't move him off of me. So needless to say I didn't win many matches in the beginning.

I eventually got tired of trying to move Ron around all the time, and I asked the instructor if I could please be paired up with someone more my size. He laughed and said "I was wondering how much longer you were going to take that before you asked." I guess he was getting a kick out of watching me struggling to move Ron Stephenson around. So he paired me up with a skinny farm boy, who weighed about the same as me and was a little shorter, and man did that make a difference. We had some great matches and the victories went back and forth. Sometimes he would win and sometimes I would win and move on the next match, but it really turned out to be fun. Coach Salmon was dedicated and a really good coach.

It turned out to be one of the best parts of going to college....at least so far.

As the fall started to turn into winter in 1966, the reality that Roger and Eddie Groves were getting closer to going to the Marine Corps became the topic of conversation at many gatherings. Also, the poker games, listening to and playing music, and generally partying in Yager's basement, was becoming a pretty common occurrence. It had become sort of a home away from home for many of us.

The Yager family, at least for me, had become almost like an extended family. Ray and Gertrude and all of Kenny and Mike's brothers and sisters treated me like a member of the family. It was always a very comfortable feeling to go there. At one point Gertrude got so used to me being there for supper she started setting a place for me and fixing extra food just in case I showed up. I think some of the fun about that was that no one could believe how much food I could eat and still be skinny as a rail.

And Gertrude was not afraid to tell you that you had responsibilities for taking advantage of her cooking. I can still hear her saying "now you boys go out and bring in some wood for this stove before you leave. You have to earn your salt around here you know." That was a small thing to do to thank her for all she did for us. And she defended her kids like any mother would.

One story that actually goes back to my senior year in high school was a rather dirty trick that Mike and I pulled on "young Kenneth" as we used to call him. Kenny had been out with some guys doing a taste test on some beers on a school night. Mike and I had been hanging out in the basement, possibly having a couple beers, but generally just listening to music and thinking of ways that we could cause "young Kenneth" some grief. We knew that when he got home that he would be in a hurry to get to bed, because as I said, it was a school night.

So Mike and I went upstairs and created some problems for Kenny. First we took every pair of shoes that we could find and stacked them in front of the bed where Kenny would get in. Next we fixed the foot of the bed so that it was at a slant, I believe we were able to unscrew the legs and take them off to accomplish that.

At that point we had apparently made enough noise that Gertrude knew what we were up to, so she hollered up through the floor vent “Now you boys quit doing things to bother Kenny. Mike you know Kenny is not going to feel very good when he gets home, so you just stop that right now.” Mike and I couldn’t contain our laughter, but we agreed that we would stop. And we did as soon as we quietly unscrewed every light bulb upstairs, including those on the stairs. And just for good measure we deposited a few more shoes on the steps. As soon as we got downstairs, we decided that it would be a good idea if Mike came to my house to spend the night, instead of being there when Kenny tried to get to bed. So Mike hollered in to Gertrude and told her that he was going home with me, and away we went. We laughed about our little stunt all the way to my house.

The next morning, my mom fixed us a quick breakfast and away we went in the old ‘58 Pontiac, headed for school. Mike was already chuckling about the fact that Kenny would have to ride the school bus. I can’t remember why he didn’t get to drive to school, anyway as we got closer to Yager’s driveway we saw Kenny standing there waiting on the bus. The closer we got, Kenny recognized my car and began to smile, because he knew we would stop and pick him up, and he wouldn't have to ride in that bumpy old school bus. However, just to complete the prank, we just honked and waved and went right on by. "Young Kenneth's" face turned from a big smile to a look of disbelief as we whizzed on by. Mike and I both laughed the rest of the way to town, all the while knowing that paybacks would be hell, but it was certainly worth it at the time. That stunt is still talked about to this day, usually with Kenny going "ha-ha ha you two were assholes" but laughing with us just the same.

By the winter of 1966 music had become a major part of the lives of many people in my generation and within my circle of friends. Kenny was playing guitar and bass guitar with the Nite Raiders band. Our classmate Elmer Zumbahlen was playing lead guitar for the time being. Our friend Jeff Dalton had been recruited to join the band, and was playing keyboards, saxophone, and was a great vocalist as well. A young man from Robinson had been auditioned for the lead guitar spot.

As soon as he started playing, he had the job. His technique and touch were already professional. His name was Greg Crouse. That wouldn't normally be a very big deal, but Greg was not your normal person coming to audition for a band. On August 9th, 1965 while riding on the back of a tractor, while a friend mowed with a bush hog, Greg fell from the tractor and before the friend could react, Greg actually went under the bush hog. His injuries were, as you can imagine, quite serious. His left hand was almost cut in two, and his left leg was almost severed at the knee. The attending surgeon told the family that he had treated a lot of young men in Viet Nam, but nothing as serious as Greg's injuries. Greg was in the hospital for several weeks, and also basically bedridden for months at home, trying to recover physically and mentally.

When Greg was injured he had never played guitar. That Christmas in 1965, Greg's parents bought Greg and his younger brother Jeff guitars and amplifiers from Sears and Roebuck. The thinking was that if Greg liked the guitar he and Jeff could take lessons and hopefully it would help Greg build strength back in his left arm and hand, and also would give him something to think about other than his horrific injuries. After a few lessons, the instructor and the family were surprised to see that Greg was actually teaching himself to play guitar, and was quickly advancing far past what the instructor had gone through in the lessons.[3]

So when Greg went back home after the audition and told his family that he was now in a band, they were all excited for Greg yet not totally surprised, because Greg was then, as he was throughout his life, one of the most determined human beings on the face of the planet. When he decided that he was going to do something, he did it. And he never did it halfheartedly.

The drummer situation for the Nite Raiders was a little less certain. The original drummer—Tony "Wop" Tripoli had moved back to the Chicago area with his family. The Nite Raiders had then auditioned a couple of drummers and decided on an underclassman named Jim Parker. He played in the high school jazz band I believe. But the Nite Raiders were doing very well, locally at least, and it was time to start widening the area. There will be much more about the Nite Raiders and other bands a little later.

So as the winter of 1966 progressed, I was struggling along with school at OCC, still a lot more concerned with women, cars, music, and parties than actually attending classes and making good grades. Also as winter swept by, the time for Roger and Eddie Groves to leave for the Marine Corps was quickly approaching.

Roger and I, along with the Woods boys—my cousins Jerry and Jag Woods—Kenny and Mike and others, were spending as much time as we could at places like Slim's and the Doghouse, local establishments in Dietrich. And although we weren't really old enough to be there, as long as we behaved ourselves and didn't act too conspicuous, we could usually stay for a while. If someone like the mayor or some other city official would happen to come in, Slim would just come over and say "alright boys it's time for you to go" and we would get the hint and leave without any delay. We would thank Slim on the way out and try our luck around the corner at the Doghouse.

The experiences at the Doghouse were usually a little more dramatic. There were usually two people there that were anything but quiet. A man known to us as "Big Jim" and a lady named Ruth. If my memory is correct, I believe that they owned the place, but I'm not 100% certain of that. Anyway you could always count on them for some action. Sometimes "Big Jim" would be angry at some guy for—let's say pulling too many bar tricks with cards, or possibly harassing Ruth over something. "Big Jim" would as loudly as he could, threaten to take them outside and beat the crap out of them, or simply grab them by the shirt and escort them to the back door and heave them out.

One such night has stuck with me for all these years. Someone had done something to irritate "Big Jim" and he was threatening to take him outside and whip him, but it was the way he was saying it that got everyone's attention. His voice was booming as he said "If you don't get the hell out of here right now, I'm gonna take you outside and stomp you in the ground—and it might take me a while—cause I've got my soft sole shoes on." The place got real quiet. Thankfully the guy got up and left. No one at our table said anything or even looked up for several minutes. We were just hoping he didn't notice us and start on us next.

At Slim's, if someone needed to leave, Slim would grab his bat or a blackjack and slam it on the bar and that usually did the trick. I never saw anyone challenge him after he had grabbed his tools.

One other memorable night at the Doghouse came on a hot day, and Ruth was dressed for comfort I suppose. She had on bib overalls without a shirt on underneath, and as she moved around the bar, reaching in the cooler for beers etc. things were coming out the side of those bibs that certainly got the attention of underage boys with hormones running like a freight train. In fact, she had the attention of everyone in the place. Even if you didn't really want, or need another beer, you were going to order one, just to stay a little longer. It was a great marketing idea, and it definitely worked.

Many times though we would simply buy some beer to go. Usually they would give us the oldest, cheapest stuff they had, but we weren't going to argue about it. We were just glad to get the goods and be on our way. Sometimes we would order quarts of beer, because they were usually cheaper in the long run. So that was our life at the time. Getting some cheap beer—getting as many people, including girls, together as you could find and go party somewhere. There was certainly still dating going on of course. I was still going out with "Lori" on a regular basis.

On or about Tuesday November 29, 1966 Roger and Eddie took a Greyhound bus to St. Louis to be there for their military physical early on the morning of Wednesday November 30. Their luggage was not packed with the typical change of underwear, clean socks, a different shirt... no their luggage was packed with beer. They checked in to a less than five star hotel—the Mark Twain hotel. In fact it may have been less than a one star. But the guys sat the beer outside the window in the cold night and began to drink it long in to the night. They passed their physical never the less and the wait was on for the next month to pass, and finally head off for their three year stent in the Marine Corps.

Tuesday December 27, 1966 was not a particularly historic or interesting day except for the fact that on Wednesday December 28th Roger and Eddie Groves were leaving for the Marine Corps. So on the evening of the 27th it was only appropriate that several of us went out to drink ourselves silly to mark the occasion.

I actually don't remember where we went, but I believe it was probably Dietrich and back to Newton, and driving around the countryside. It's been long enough that I don't remember who drove that night, but some of the cars—including Roger's—were left at Dick's Marathon. Sometime pretty late at night we arrived back at Dick's Marathon to say our goodbye's and best wishes to Roger. As we were about to get in our cars and leave, someone else showed up to join the party. It was our "old friend" State Trooper Robert Copper. He stepped up to our group and asked "what the hell are all you guys doing here." No one said anything for a few seconds and finally to break the tension Roger spoke up and said, rather sloppily, "I'm gettin' ready to go to the Marine Corps." Trooper Copper, a former Marine, began laughing out loud--I mean he couldn't control himself. When he finally got his laughter under control, he said "Kinder-you wouldn't make a pimple on a Marine's ass." Well, speaking just for myself, I didn't know whether to laugh or just bite my tongue. I chose the latter. Roger just said "well I'm leaving tomorrow anyway." Trooper Copper still chuckling said something to the effect of "God help us all" and then he said "All right you guys, you all get the hell out of here and out of town, or I'll give you a ticket for illegal consumption." We didn't waste any time doing exactly what Mr. Copper had suggested.

So, the next day Sharon Michl, our friend from high school, drove Roger and Eddie to the Greyhound bus station in Effingham for their departure to St. Louis. Let me add at this point that to this day no one is sure why either Roger's parents or Eddie's parents or I or another close friend of Eddie's didn't drive them to the bus station. But Sharon handled the responsibility just fine, and they were off to become Marines. They were sworn in and inducted in St. Louis, then off to Kansas City for a brief stop and on to San Diego. One other quick note. The same day that Roger and Eddie left Jasper County for the Marine Corps, two other young men left with them, class of '66 member Jerry Swisher and class of '65 member Bob Albright. Those two would be in boot camp and actually in the same platoon with Roger and Eddie. Once they reached the airport in San Diego, they were all bussed over to the United States Marine Corps Recruit Depot. That's where all the "fun" begins. The lives of Roger and Eddie would never be the same again. I have heard from several Marines that you then become whatever form of excrement, vomit, or waste material that your drill sergeant says that you are.

So the boys were gone, and the parade of young men headed to the military from Jasper County was well under way. The U. S. military had a big appetite and it needed to be fed. And even though all of us had been trying to wash away the fact that the war in Viet Nam was getting closer to home, it didn't work. And the ringing in our ears just got a little louder.

Part Three

A Change in Wind Direction

The winter days of early 1967 were a turning point in my life. Days at OCC were still not really a priority for me, but I was at least making the effort to do well, as least in the classes that interested me. My algebra teacher, Mr. Pixley, taught well enough to keep my attention, and I mean that with all due respect. He was very good at challenging people to do their best or at least do better. I think I got a C in his class which for me was pretty good considering that I was usually very poor at math.

The other good thing about math class was I got to sit by a very pretty and smart girl whose name was Becky. She was very sharp, in a lot of ways, but we were just friends, and I knew that was as far as it would go because all she could talk about was her boyfriend Terry, and his car.

His car was a red 1963 Chevy Impala Super Sport. It had deep dish chrome reverse wheels on the back and Astro mags on the front. It was extremely sharp, and always immaculately shined. I used to see it pull in the parking lot of OCC daily, and just stare at it. I didn't really know Terry personally, but I knew he had a good thing going, because all the "goodies" that the car had were purchased by Becky. She had bought him the wheels, the chrome valve covers, the chrome air breather cover, the Hurst linkage, a custom red metal flake steering wheel—that was much smaller than the stock one. It made the car easier to handle. So, like I said he had a good thing going.

The reason that I know about her buying all the stuff is she was just as proud of the car as he was, and she liked buying him stuff for it for birthdays, Christmas, Valentine's Day etc. And she was happy to talk about it. I told her in class one day—actually I may have had two classes with her—that if Terry ever traded that car off to please let me know, and she said that she would. So as you can see I had a reason to go to at least a couple of classes.

Also that winter, I went into speech class one day and sat down by a guy that I hadn't seen before. I introduced myself to him and found out his name was Monty Blair. He was, unbeknownst to me, actually from Newton. His mom Jan worked for Thermogas as a receptionist/secretary. Thermogas was the local propane distributor, owned at the time by Roe Griffith and—if memory serves me correctly—Jim Yates. Blair and I became friends almost instantly. I'll explain why we bonded so quickly a little later.

That winter was also the start of my being much more involved in music. I had known for a long time that I wanted to play drums. My parents actually bought a little toy drum kit for me when I was probably ten years old. I think they were hoping that would keep me in the basement playing on them, instead of dragging out my mom's pots and pans on the kitchen floor, and banging on them with spoons. It worked for about two days. The heads on that little drum kit were made of some really thin plastic, along with the "shells" of really thin metal. I beat them into oblivion within just a couple of days.

Later on as I got in to my early teens, I would approach drummers at dances—at teen centers and so forth—and ask them if they had any broken or old drumsticks that I could have. Once I got those, I would sit on the corner of my bed, and beat the daylights out of the bed, while listening to records on my old Sears Arvin stereo.

Later that winter I found out that my old friend Alan Beard had a set of drums. He wasn't playing in a band, so from time to time I would ask him if I could borrow them, and just practice. Alan was very good about letting me do that.

The only place I could set up Alan's kit was in the concession stand at the Fairview Drive In. The concession stand was a block building with a concrete floor. So the sounds of me practicing were very loud in our house, which was some 100 yards away. My parents would tell me that they had to turn the T.V. up to almost maximum volume, just to hear their programs. We were not open during the winter at that time, so I didn't have to worry about tearing the kit down every night. And after a few days, I would take Alan's drums back to him.

After a few times of borrowing Alan's drums, I told my parents "hey you know if I owned a set of drums I could probably get in a band and would be able to pay for them." My parents responded that I should get in the band first and then spend the money for a drum kit. I couldn't really argue that point, because I really didn't have an income at the time, and not much in savings. Going to OCC and living at home did have some advantages of course, but no income was a real bummer. But I had the bug so bad to have my own drum kit that I asked Alan one day if he would be interested in selling his kit. My memory is that he didn't want to at the time, but after I asked a couple more times, he said that he would. We agreed on $75.00.

His kit was a silver sparkle, five piece Slingerland kit with no hi-hat, and I believe it only had one cymbal with it. But I didn't care. I was about to own my own drum kit. I went to the bank and pulled the $75.00 out of savings, and gave it to Alan. He was happy to get the money, and I was thrilled to have a drum kit. I loaded them in to my trusty '58 Pontiac and headed for home.

As thrilled as I was, my parents were a lot less excited. But I promised them that I would get in a band one way or another. I was eighteen, it wasn't like I couldn't spend any money without asking first, but my parents grew up during the depression and buying something like a drum kit, with no definite plans for it was something they probably would have never done. So I told Kenny and Mike and all my other buddies, that I finally had a drum kit.

During that winter, for some reasons I guess I never really knew, the Nite Raiders were having trouble getting their drummer to show up for scheduled practice sessions. Those practice sessions were held in the basement of Yager's house. So once I had a drum kit, I was invited to come over and practice with the band, so they could continue to learn new songs, and hopefully get more gigs. I was more than happy to do that, because it gave me a chance to practice and learn new songs as well. And maybe one step closer to actually playing in a band. I had also added a few new pieces to the drum kit—a hi-hat stand and cymbals, another crash cymbal and stand. It was beginning to sound a lot better.

And then one evening while Kenny, Mike and I were just hanging out in the basement listening to music, Kenny got a call from Gene Hartke, the owner/operator of the Crystal Club near Effingham. Gene told Kenny that the band for that night—either a Friday or Saturday night—had cancelled at the last minute, and he wanted to know if Kenny could get a band together and come to the Crystal to play that night. This was approximately three hours before the band would normally start.

So Kenny looks around at Mike and me and says "hey do you guys want to go play at the Crystal tonight?" "The band cancelled on him." Well Mike and I had about 20 seconds to make a decision. We had jammed a little bit in the basement with Kenny and the Nite Raiders and other people that would show up with instruments, but none of us had ever played together as a group, and certainly not out on a real gig, in front of a large crowd. So naturally Mike and I said "sure we'll go." So Kenny tells Gene Hartke that we'll be there to play. So now in the next couple of hours we have to get some more guys together, get over to Effingham, and play some decent songs at a bar that expects to hear decent live music from people that know what they're doing.

So the scramble was on to get people, equipment and songs together for an actual paying job. My memory and time have clouded the makeup of the guys who went that night. Kenny, Mike and I grabbed our equipment and loaded it in our cars. I think Jeff Dalton was available, but other than that I don't remember the entire group, but we all made it to the Crystal about 30 minutes before we were due to start. There was really no time to get nervous. We probably knew 12 to 15 songs between us. Typically a band doesn't go out to play gigs until they know at least 40 songs and can maybe fake another 10. But there we were, in front of a big crowd expecting to hear a professional band. After we had played a few songs the fear and nervousness started to fade a little. The crowd actually seemed to like what we were doing. So we got done with the first set, having pretty much played all the songs that we actually knew, and went to get a beer to settle our nerves a little more. Gene Hartke must have told the bar staff that it was ok to serve us, because at that point, no one was old enough to get served, with the exception of Jeff Dalton, and he didn't drink alcohol.

The next three sets were interesting. We were supposed to play until 1:00 a.m. So needless to say we had to repeat songs. We got requests, some of which we actually played, and somehow we actually made it through, and at the end of the night Gene was very appreciative and we got payed. A paying gig in front of a large crowd. I was hooked right then and there.

Not long after the thrown together gig at the Crystal Club, and the fact that the Nite Raiders drummer problems had continued, I was asked to be the regular drummer for the Nite Raiders. To say that I was excited would be an understatement. I had gone from borrowing a drum kit from my friend Alan Beard to practice on, to owning a drum kit, and now finally I was in a band. This was a game changer for me. Every "wanna be" musician had dreamed of being in a band as soon as they heard their first Beatles song, and certainly after they saw them, and the reaction to them, on the Ed Sullivan Show. I now had a direction besides cars, women and drinking beer. This was something to be proud of and to work toward being better, and more importantly, being able to work with good friends and good musicians to achieve something that most people either could not or would not do.

When I told my parents about being in a band, they were thrilled for me as well. They probably knew also that my having a hobby that was going to pay for itself was a good thing for all concerned. So the Nite Raiders then consisted of Kenny Yager, Greg Crouse, Elmer Zumbahlen, Jeff Dalton, and me. We were all friends, we got along great, and the gigs were starting to come in pretty regularly. And the practice sessions continued in Yager's basement on a regular basis. The Viet Nam war was certainly still raging, but for now it was a distant rumble. We had different things to think about.

My friend Monty Blair drove an old 1954 Chevy. It was a green two door sedan, and he called it "the frog". But it got him back and forth to OCC and that's all he cared about. He took any good natured ribbing about his cars appearance with his usual come back, "complaints! Hey it runs doesn't it?" It gets me there and back doesn't it? What more do I need?" Blair—which is what most everyone called him—didn't need a lot or ever expect to have a lot.

He and his mom Jan lived in a very meager mobile home on west Sycamore Street. (I think) His father had left them when Blair was very young. His mom's family was from the Olney area, and Jan was remarried to a man from that area. The second husband turned out to be an alcoholic and a con artist who was pretty good at cheating people out of their money and writing bad checks. His name was Don Hayes. That game caught up to him at some point, and he was incarcerated in Menard Correctional Center (Southern Illinois Penitentiary) in Chester, IL.

So Blair's life had been anything but smooth, but he rarely complained about anything. Before I ever knew anything about his step-father being in prison, I would notice Blair sketching a picture, while we were in speech class, of a man sitting cross legged on the floor behind bars. At first, when I would ask him about it—what did it mean—he would just say "oh it's just the way I feel sometimes." The more I got to know Blair, the more I realized that it probably did have a dual meaning to it. Blair didn't complain verbally about very much, but he did have his ways of letting you know how he was feeling.

And Blair certainly didn't want to hear about people feeling sorry for themselves. I can remember a number of times saying something to the effect that "man I wish I had more money to do this or that" and Blair's classic comeback of "Complaints! If I could go around the world on a dollar, hell I couldn't leave the porch." It was Blair's humorous, but subtle way of saying stop your complaining. Sometimes I would complain just to hear him go off on me with his standard comeback. Blair and I became very close friends, and we shared a lot of feelings—mostly good, but some bad. We were both searching for a direction, but I at least had a solid family situation and eventually had the band to take up a lot of my time. More about Blair and our adventures a little later.

I walked into my math class one afternoon and took my usual seat beside Becky. After some typical chatter, she looks up and says "oh by the way, my boyfriend traded his 63 Super Sport off yesterday. He got a new Chevelle SS 396." I know my mouth had to have fallen completely open. I said "you're kidding me, where did he trade it in?" She says "I think it was up in Newton." I said "are you sure, you mean at Al Rohr Chevrolet?" She said "Yeah I'm just sure that's where he had ordered it from." Well I know I couldn't concentrate through the rest of the math class, and I don't remember what class or classes I had after math class, but I know I skipped them and got myself back to Al Rohr Chevrolet as fast as I could.

My recollection is that, "Beef" Kinsel was just backing it out of the garage area when I pulled in. I parked immediately and was standing there when he opened the door to get out. I said "Man I can't believe you have this car here" and "Beef" says "yeah it's a dandy isn't it, yeah it's a dandy. You wanna buy it Ronnie?" I said "are you kidding, of course I want to buy it. How much are you asking for it?" He said "well we just got it in—I think he's (he being Al Rohr) got $1395.00 on it Ronnie, let me go check." Well at this point "Beef" knew he had a live one on the line, as I was like a little kid in a candy store looking in the jar asking "how much for that big red lollipop?" Sure enough he came back and told me that it was priced at $1395.00. At that point I knew I needed a more experienced negotiator to work on this deal. That would be my dad. So I told "Beef" that I would be back as soon as I could. So I hopped back in the old ‘58 Pontiac, and took off for home as fast as I could. It’s possible that I was speeding on the way home.

I found my dad in his office working, and I excitedly told him that I had just looked at a car that I knew all about, because I sat by this girl in math class and.... At that point my dad says “hold it—slow down a little here. I’ve got work to do right now, maybe we can go look at it tomorrow.” I said “no—we can’t wait until tomorrow, if that car is sitting out on the lot, twenty other guys are gonna be in there looking at it.”

So with a little mumbling and maybe a little cussing, he got up—called over to the house to let my mom know we were going to Newton to look at a car—and away we go. I told him as much as I could think of about the car on the way. My old ‘58 Pontiac was still in pretty good shape, although it did have a damaged bumper and right rear quarter panel from an accident that I had on the way home from school one afternoon. Other than that it was still very sound, and pretty darn fast for just your basic two door hardtop Pontiac. So we found “Beef Kinsel, and my dad began looking the car over, and asking me questions. “Beef” was making comments like “yeah she’s a beauty ain’t she Lamar, yeah she’s a beauty all right.” “Beef” had a habit of repeating himself, but he was a really nice man. He was just your standard issue car salesman. Basically he would just let you sell yourself, and agree with you as you did it.

I could tell that even my dad was pretty impressed with the car. It was always immaculately clean. I'm sure Rohr's didn't have to do anything to it, as far as cleaning it. So the negotiations started between my dad and "Beef." Back and forth. Talking about my car on a trade and what would have to be done to it etc. Finally "Beef" says "Well boys here's what we can do. We'll take a thousand dollars difference and your car for it, and that's the best we can do. That Chevy will sell in a couple of days, one way or the other."

Even though my dad knew he was right, he said "now wait a minute "Beef" a thousand dollars is a lot of money, I just don't think we can do that." So now my head is about to explode. I was going to be the one paying for the car anyway, but I didn't say anything. "Beef" says "well Lamar Ronnie's car is good, but it's gonna have to go in the body shop first, before we can sell it, so that's the best we can do." My dad looked at me and said "well you're going to be the one making the payments on it, so I guess if you want it that bad we'll go ahead with it." I was ecstatic. Man I had dreamed about owning that car from the first time I had seen it, and certainly after talking to Becky about it practically every day. At least one thing about going to OCC had really worked out.

The next day my dad went with me to talk to Mr. Pickerel about the new car. Again he assured him that the payments were to be made by me. Mr. Pickerel agreed to do the note, and congratulated me on the new ride. I was so happy I could have floated out of the bank. Later that afternoon, I was driving the car that I had been drooling over for months. At that moment, life was very good.

The Nite Raiders band was beginning to improve a lot, and we were getting a lot more opportunities to play. Although we were still playing teen dances of one sort or another, we were playing in different towns and from time to time, we got to play in bars and clubs. One of the reasons that we were improving so much is that we practiced regularly. My best memory is that we practiced on Wednesday nights. Our goal was to continue to learn the most popular songs from radio top 40, and some of the album cuts that we knew the kids liked.

Band practice usually always attracted other people as well. Friends that knew we were practicing, both boys and girls, would stop in to hear what we were learning. A few beers would be shared, and it usually worked out fine unless the visitors got too disruptive. Kenny and Mike's mom—Gertrude—was such a patient lady when it came to all the people showing up for band practice, and she never complained about it. She would typically just go upstairs and turn on the TV and let whatever was going on in the basement, just go on.

During the winter and early spring of 1967 other musicians were showing up in Yager's basement too. They said that they were forming a band, and would soon be playing gigs, and giving the Nite Raiders some competition. That wouldn't have been a big deal at all, except for the fact that one of those musicians was Kenny's brother Mike. Yeah, my good friend, beer drinking buddy, and fellow music nut, was forming a band to give us a run for our money. That group would consist of Mike Yager, Larry Reich, Jim Logan, and Artie Hunzinger. Eventually they would decide on the name The Illusions.

Actually we—The Nite Raiders—thought that it was pretty cool that they had decided to start a band, the more young talent and energy on the music scene the better. There was one minor problem however. Where were they going to practice? Well if you guessed that they too would be practicing in Yager's basement, you are correct. It's been too many years to remember who practiced on what night, or if we switched nights from time to time, but at least two nights a week a band, playing some pretty loud rock and roll music was in the basement.

You now can understand why I proclaimed how patient Gertrude Yager was. And sometimes Ray would have a night off, and he would be there too. No matter how long or loud we played, I swear they never complained. Gertrude would later say that honestly, it never bothered her, plus if her boys were in the basement playing music, she didn't have to wonder where they were. She and Ray were amazing.

The Illusions developed a really tight sound very quickly. Also after much thought and conversation about the marketing of the band, they decided to emulate, as closely as they could, the very popular national recording artist Paul Revere and the Raiders. They didn't have the actual colonial coats, but they wore the high black boots, and double breasted jackets. No one had any difficulty in knowing who they wanted to look like, and they looked sharp. The "competition" between the two bands was friendly, and really it was a lot more like comradery among musicians. We were having a blast, and everyone was constantly trying to get better.

Sometimes depending on the number of gigs coming up one or both of the bands would practice an additional night. It was crazy. It was almost like a non-stop rehearsal schedule, and then you would go play jobs on the weekends. No one was complaining though, that's what being in a band was all about. It's what we all had dreamed about. We were all pretty much immersed in our own little musical world. There were jobs, and school, and personal responsibilities of course but speaking for myself, they were secondary to the rather euphoric atmosphere going on around the band and the fact that I had a new car that was awesome. Also, as far as dating goes, my attention had definitely turned to "Ruby."

I was certainly interested in my little corner of the world, but if my parents needed help at the Drive-In or my aunt Fern needed something done that I could handle, or my grandma Woods needed transported from town to our house I would certainly do it. Naturally teen age priorities are different than parents or the other adults in your life, but I don't want to leave the impression that my friends I and were total selfish slobs, and didn't care about anyone else. That was certainly not the case.

Once the weather was warm enough Blair brought his motorcycle out of the storage shed. When I found out that he had a motorcycle, of course I wanted to see it and ride it. If my memory serves me well, it was a 1962 Ducati. It wasn't made for the track, so I believe it would have been a Monza 250cc. It wasn't perfect, but it was pretty nice. It had been down a couple of times and the tank and the fenders were a little beat up, but it was very rideable. It was at times though a little touchy, as far as the carburetor was concerned. Much of our time working on the bike was spent trying to get the fuel mixture correct, but we were having fun with it, and actually that's pretty much all we cared about at the time.

I guess it was about that time that I found out that Blair could only see out of his left eye. Oh he had a bit of vision in his right eye, but very little. He would have been automatically 4-F for the military, unable to serve. But as usual Blair never really complained about his vision, and I was never sure why he didn't wear glasses all the time. Also once the motorcycle hill climbing season started, Blair and I went to as many "climbs" as we could find in the area. Mostly it was a place near Neoga. And once we saw what it took to climb those hills, we had an idea for Blair's bike. We would try to transform it from a street bike, which it definitely was, to something we could take to the country and have some fun climbing hills. We didn't have any illusion about being able to enter the actual competition, but maybe we could find some nice hills to climb in the Newton area.

Eventually we started the transformation on the Ducati. The first thing to go was the tail light and part of the rear fender. My best memory is that we took the fender off and used a hack saw to cut it basically in half and reattached the remaining half. Rear fenders and tail lights would only be in the way if you got in to some serious off road fun. On a different day we totally removed the front fender.

And on a different day that summer we removed the head light assembly. It was a rather bulky headlight, and I assume that we must have thought that it was weight we didn't need, and besides real hill climbers didn't have headlights anyway. The bike was now officially not street legal, but we still rode it in town from time to time, and honestly I don't know how we made it without getting stopped by either state or local police. We were just lucky I guess. Or maybe not.

Part Four

The Wind Speed Increases

After the Illusions had so successfully branded themselves, and were improving weekly and getting more jobs, the Nite Raiders were also looking for ideas to "brand" the band and have a recognizable feature, in order to attract both the teen audience and for the slightly older audiences that would be in the bars and clubs and possibly the college crowd.

During that time, Kenny and or Greg had been contacted by a booking agent from Indiana about the possibility of him booking the band for several jobs in Indiana. He came to listen to us play at some point, and told us that he really liked us and if we could just learn some more songs by the Beach Boys, he could probably get us a lot of gigs in Indiana. Well, we were already doing some of the Beach Boys songs and not many other local or regional bands were doing a lot of the Beach Boys music, so we unanimously decided that we would become the central Illinois version of the Beach Boys.

At that time the Beach Boys were all dressing alike in their promo shots. One of the favorites was the striped shirts and white pants look from the early 1964 and 1965 photos and appearances. My memory has faded a bit on this, but we found or ordered red and white striped shirts and white pants for everyone at Gene's Men's Wear, on the south side of the square in Newton. Gene Reich, who owned the clothing store, was the father of Larry Reich, the keyboard player and vocalist for the Illusions. I can only assume that Gene outfitted the Illusions as well.

So we had our new look, and hopes for a number of new jobs in the Indiana market. We did indeed get a few new places to play in that market, but the additional travel expenses, plus the booking agent got a percentage (typically 10%) of the payout for the band, so the benefits were not necessarily worth the additional effort. But the new look was a hit never the less. It "fit" us for the type of music we were playing at the time.

We didn't end up doing a lot of Beach Boys material, but more than most bands. The Beatles were still putting out so much new material that we had to do as much of it as we could. Plus we were certainly doing a lot of the Chicago bands material, Cryan' Shames, New Colony Six,

Buckinghams, etc. Naturally the national and international groups were extremely popular, but for downstate Illinois, the Chicago bands were big. So the Nite Raiders were playing a lot of gigs, the Illusions were playing a lot as well, and the weekly practice sessions in Yager's basement continued on a regular basis. I think I can safely say that both bands were very happy with the way things were going.

Because of the band schedule, I really didn't want to commit my night time hours to my parents at the Fairview Drive-In. I was certainly willing to help with the ongoing projects and chores during the daytime, but my dad needed someone to work during the day and could also commit to working three or four nights a week at the box office. That was just the nature of the business. So, my dad and I came to the understanding that I would have to get full time employment elsewhere, but I could still live at home. I don't remember how it all came about, but I found out about an opening at Dick's Marathon, possibly from my uncle Wayne. He was a Marathon oil product distributer for the area. Anyway, I went in to talk to Dick Tracy about it, and he hired me.

It was definitely a full time job. Six days a week and eventually every third Sunday 'til noon. But

Dick was always very good about letting you off for a day if you really needed to go somewhere or had a family emergency. So I had a full time job, the band was cooking along very nicely, Blair and I were having a blast riding his Ducati, and the parties were plentiful. What more could a Jasper County boy ask for in the summer of '67? Well maybe one more thing.

I had also been seeing "Ruby" at some of the parties and one thing led to another and we had started dating on a regular basis. That made for a very busy, crazy, and wild summer. It was so busy that you could almost forget there was a war going on, but not quite.

Later that summer, I suppose sometime in July, the Nite Raiders got confirmation that we were going to be playing on one of the talent stages at the Illinois State Fair. I seem to remember that it was Jeff Dalton who had made the contact and was in charge of getting us there on time. Also about that time Kenny got an invitation from the U.S. Army to please go take a physical to see if he qualified to join them for some activities that were going on about 6,800 miles away. That's not exactly how it was worded, but we all knew what the message really meant.

It was certainly a bitter sweet time, but the reality of what was about to happen was clear. As it turned out, Kenny was indeed qualified to be a member of the Army, and his date of departure was Monday, August 14. The Nite Raiders would play at the State Fair on Saturday August 12. We didn't want to talk about it, we didn't want to think about it, but the wind wouldn't stop blowing. The ringing in our ears was getting louder all the time. That wicked damn thing called reality was creeping back into our lives—relentlessly.

It wasn't just the band members and friends who were concerned about Kenny's upcoming departure for the Army. Naturally the entire Yager family was upset and concerned. But like the rest of us, they were trying not to talk about it or think about it. Everyone put a smile on their faces and just acknowledged what the facts were and went on with their lives the best they could. This same scenario was going on in households, not only in Jasper County, but in hundreds of thousands of homes across the country. Most of those homes supported what the U.S. military was trying to accomplish.

Most had seen or heard about the ruthless tactics that the Viet Cong used on their own people to try and gain support for the communists and the North

Vietnamese army. It was guerilla warfare. Not something that, before Viet Nam, the U.S. had encountered or fought against on any large scale. And the brutality of the war was being shown to us on the evening news every day. And don't forget, there were a lot of young women serving in Viet Nam as well, many in supporting roles and many as nurses. Thank goodness for the nurses, and for the surgeons. It was not a pleasant time for any of them either.

The night before the Nite Raiders were to head off to the State Fair, I had an appointment with one of the best Chevrolet mechanics in the country to put a different cam in my '63 Super Sport. Alan Dale Wetherholt was widely known to be the "go to guy" if you needed something done to your Chevy engine. I had ordered the cam myself and asked Alan if he would do the job. He agreed to do it at his house, if I would help him. He had left Dan Hecht Chevrolet in Effingham as a mechanic because the solvents used to clean parts were so rough on his hands that they would become raw and painful. So I agreed that I would clean and wash whatever needed to be done to help him.

Of course I supplied the gasket and seal kits as well. Some of my band mates were concerned that my car would not be available on Saturday. Their thoughts were that maybe we would get the car torn down and not be able to finish it in one night. They were just unaware of Alan Dale's talent. The reason for the cam change was that it would add another 20 to 25 horsepower. It was the hydraulic cam used in the 350 horsepower Chevy engines. So I took a couple of six packs, the cam, and maybe $20.00 bucks and headed down to Alan Dale's place near Latona or Dog Town as it was known locally. The job went really fast. Under Alan Dale's experienced hands and direction we got it torn down, cleaned up and put back together within about three hours, and admittedly there was a little bit of beer drinking going on during that time.

Once we were totally finished, Alan Dale said "there's just one more thing I want to do to this car before you leave." I said "what's that?" He said "drive it." I said "You got it, let's go." So we drove just north of Latona on the black top and he stopped, revved it up to about three thousand rpm's and popped the clutch. The car was always pretty fast, but the addition of the new cam was evident right away. Alan Dale wound it up to 5200 rpm's in all four gears, the red line for the small block, and it didn't float the valves. (Car guys will know what I'm talking about) Alan Dale had a big smile on his face. He said "that's exactly what I wanted to see, that cam is doing what it's supposed to do." So just for good measure he had to do it a couple more times before we went back to his house. I was thrilled, and Alan Dale was too. We both had big smiles on our face.

Admittedly it was a little late when I got home, but I didn't care, it was mission completed for me. I loaded my drums in the car, and tried to get some sleep. I had to "change gears" now. It was going to be a long and busy day for the Nite Raiders on Saturday, longer than we could have ever imagined.

Although we knew how to get to the State Fair grounds and had some idea what gate to go through, many, many other people were also trying to get there. The traffic on Dirksen Parkway was creeping along at a snail's pace. Even when we finally got up to North Grand, it was a mess. We had three or four vehicles full of people and equipment and we were now running late. After what seemed like hours, we made it to the gate we were supposed to enter through. We all found a parking spot, but the problem was we weren't sure where the stage was located or who we were supposed to report to. Other than that, everything was going smoothly.

Most of us headed down toward the building where a lot of the Fair offices were located. Greg stayed behind with the equipment. Greg had a brace on his left leg to help support his knee, from his previous injury. He could walk and get around just fine, but it was a long trek through the fairgrounds just to get to the offices. And of course this was long before cell phones. Finally we found someone who seemed to know what we were talking about, and directed us to the correct stage.

It was at the intersection of two main roads within the fairgrounds, and this stage happened to be sponsored by Bunny Bread. We made our way back to the cars and equipment, and started trying to make our way through the people with our cars, trying to get close enough to the stage to start unloading equipment and set up. It was organized chaos getting all the equipment set up, plugged in, tested, doing a half-assed sound check, getting the cars back out to the parking lot, changing into our Beach Boys clothes, and getting ready to start our first set on the Bunny Bread stage.

By the time we got ready to start we were already hungry and thirsty and half worn out, but we were also very excited. And then the Bunny Bread sponsors representative showed up. It was Miss Bunny Bread. She had on your basic "Daisy Duke" shorts, a crisp white short sleeved blouse, she was blond, buxom, probably 22 or 23 years old, and had a great personality to go with it. Man we were all glad to see her. The day just got a lot better.

After introducing herself to the band, she explained that she would be there most of the time, and that she would introduce us to the crowd before each set. We would play for about 30 minutes at a time, take about a 20 minute break and then do another 30 minute set. We were scheduled to do that until about 6:00 o'clock in the evening.

During the breaks, besides getting something to eat or drink, the band would sit down on the front of the stage and talk to people from the crowd and sign autographs. Yeah....four guys from Jasper County and one from Crawford County signing autographs at the State Fair. Also, Miss Bunny Bread was signing pictures of herself for the crowd. She had been a third runner-up in a Miss America pageant a couple of years before, and knew how to handle a crowd. The day turned out to be a very long and tiring day, but it was also a blast. Not that many bands got to do what we were doing. And being able to tell prospective club and bar owners or people in charge of various teen centers, that we had played at the State Fair was a plus for sure.

Once all the equipment was taken down and loaded, and we had all said our goodbye's to Miss Bunny Bread, some of us headed home and some headed for a party in Springfield. Some girls from Newton and Jasper County were working and living in Springfield and as it turned out were having a party that night. As tired as I was, a place to clean up and have some cold beer sounded really good. Also, some other friends and acquaintances from Newton and the surrounding area had made the trip up for both the State Fair and the party. It was rowdy. A rather drunken good time was had by all. It went on long into the morning.

The next day, I believe I remember that some of us went to get some breakfast before the trip home. On the way home Kenny and I laughed and talked about the day and night before, and tried not to talk at all about the fact that on Monday morning, August the 14th, 1967, he was headed off to a different kind of party. He would no longer be a member of a rock band, or a civilian—he was on his way to Fort Leonard Wood, MO for basic training. Also leaving that morning were classmates Gene Koebele, Mike Smith and Mike Michl. The list of Jasper County draftees continued to grow, and it wouldn't be letting up any time soon.

On Sunday August 13, 1967, there was a going away party for Kenny at Kenny Ray and Kathleen Tate's house. Kathleen (Kate) was Kenny's older sister. They lived just east of Yager's on Lake Jasper. Both the Illusions and the Nite Raiders played music that day. We shared equipment and sat up on the front porch of the house. Many family members were there. Friends of all the band members showed up and we all drank beer and ate some great food, and gave Kenny a great send off. It was a bitter sweet day. No one knew the next time we'd all be together like this, or if we ever would.

My working "partner" at Dick's Marathon in the summer and fall of 1967 was Norbert "Nort" Wagner. He was the brother of a friend and classmate of mine, Dick Wagner. "Nort" was probably five years older than me, and with all due respect, he was not the brightest bulb in the lamp, but we did work together fairly well. There were, however, times when we would just rub each other the wrong way, and the words would begin flying, and the tempers would amp up, and then the fists would begin to fly as well. The fight never lasted very long though, because at the first sign of a fist fight, Dick would be in the middle of it, telling us to knock it off and get back to work.

Probably the most notable fight came after a long night of playing music and partying, for me and the Nite Raiders, in Robinson. I got home very late, actually early in the morning, and blundered into work on that Saturday morning with a massive hang over and headache. At the time, Dick's Marathon was known as the best place to get a car wash, and car detailing. Dick absolutely demanded quality work and he would "white glove" your work before it was released to go back to the customer. The wash room was busy from open to close. And "Nort" and I were also responsible for gas customers and other things that needed done. The point being, there was much work to do, and not really any time for foolishness.

At about 9:00 am, I was working in the wash bay, trying to get a mud caked fender skirt off a car, which was always a miserable, knuckle busting job. As I was squatted down at the right rear wheel well, cursing the mud and the rusty lever under it—BOOM—a firecracker went off under the car. After the initial shock, I went flying around the car looking for "Nort", who was now dying laughing on the other side of the car. He had to know what was coming next.

By the time I got to him, he had already assumed his fighting position. I got in a couple really good shots to his jaw, before he landed one on the side of my head. As I was about to go in for another swing, Dick showed up to put an end to the whole thing. He stepped in the middle of us, and said something to the effect that, neither one of us could fight our way out of a wet paper bag, or how pitiful we were at fighting etc. He did remind "Nort" that there was a lot of flammable material in the area, and that better be the last firecracker that ever went off in the station. He also told me to get my butt back to work.

I told "Nort" that it wasn't over, and he hurled a couple insults back at me, and we went back to work. I knew that I would get my chance at revenge in the coming days. Actually I didn't have to wait very long, and as it turned out I didn't have to do anything.

Later that afternoon as "Nort" was backing a car out of the wash bay, for whatever reason, he had the driver side door open somewhat, and before anyone could say anything—he drove the car door right in to the wash bay door frame. The car door buckled and the hinges popped. "Nort" slammed the car back in to drive and pulled forward. The look on his face said it all. I didn't dare laugh, because I knew what was coming next. Dick unleashed a tirade on "Nort" that actually made me feel a little bit sorry for him. The tongue lashing went on for several minutes before Dick finally let up on him and went to call the customer to let him know what had happened.

Man what a day it had been. And that evening I went home to clean up and get ready for another gig with the Nite Raiders. It was time to forget the day and get ready to entertain people with some good rock and roll music, drink a couple cold beers, and let the good times roll.

Many times during that summer and fall, "Ruby" would go with me to gigs. I didn't mind that at all, because I frankly wanted to spend as much time with her as possible. Of course once we got to the gig, I had to go to work. "Ruby" would usually find a place relatively close to the band to sit and watch. Now in full disclosure, she always attracted a lot of attention. Any red-blooded American boy with a pulse wanted to dance with her, or at least sit and talk to her. And to "Ruby's" credit, she would come and ask me if it was ok if she danced with whoever was snooping around, and most of the time I didn't have a problem with it. I knew that at the end of the gig, she was going home with me. Truthfully, I had it made. I had a beautiful girlfriend, I was playing in a very good and popular rock band, I had a really nice car, and I had a job that allowed me to do that. It was one of the best times of my life, and I really wanted it to go on forever.

When Kenny left for the army, it obviously left a hole in the lineup for the Nite Raiders. But as was mentioned earlier, Greg's younger brother Jeff Crouse also got a guitar for Christmas at the same time as Greg. He may not have learned as quickly as Greg did, but he had gotten very proficient on guitar, and he could also do a very good job with backing vocals, so Jeff joined our band. With Greg's help and a lot of practice, he became a very important part of the band.

Jeff also brought a bit of naivete' to the band as well, because he had never experienced anything like it before. His energy was a very welcome addition, considering we could never really replace Kenny. It was really fun to watch Jeff develop. I swear he even had fun carrying in equipment.

One night Jeff was in Newton hanging out with me, and having a couple beers. We were driving around Newton talking about things that two teenage boys would talk about......girls, music, beer, girls, music, girls.....well you get the idea. When I bought the '63 Chevy Super Sport, it had dual glass pack mufflers. If you have forgotten about glass packs--as they got older—they got a lot louder. At the time, it was really cool to wind the car up in say, second gear, and let off the gas and listen to the glass packs rack. They would pop and carry on for several seconds each time.

So Jeff and I had been having a good time doing that on several streets around Newton, while having a beer now and then. As we were heading back towards the square, after doing the turnaround at Neese's station, on the south end of Van Buren Street, I noticed a cop car swing in behind me about the time we were passing the grade school. He didn't turn his red lights on though, he just followed me up to the square. I got in the right lane, and was getting ready to turn towards the Dog-n-Suds, when "Doc" Jourdan pulled up beside me, and stopped.

His window was down already, and he leaned over and said "Kinder-you've got 'til sundown tomorrow night to get those glass packs off that car." "If I catch you with them on after that, I'll give you a ticket—do you understand?" I just said, "Yes I understand." "Doc" pulled away, and Jeff and I went on our way, feeling like we had just been warned by Marshall Dillion to get out of town. It was actually funny, but I took old "Doc" seriously, and the next day I went to Newton Auto Parts, purchased two new mufflers and tail pipes, and after working hours, I put my car on the lift and installed my new exhaust system. Truthfully, as soon as I started the car with the stock mufflers on, I really liked it. It was so much quieter. So in a way old "Doc" Jourdan did me a favor, in more ways than one. He could have given me the ticket and still made me change mufflers. I guess that was one advantage of living in a small town.

I was 19 years old, living the good life, and I was in a "serious" relationship with "Ruby." When you're young and think that you know everything about everything, it's hard to realize that maybe you're moving a little too fast. "Ruby" was still only 17, but there had already been some discussion of getting married. It seemed like the right thing to do at the time. We would have to wait until the following summer, until "Ruby" turned 18, but so what, we could do that....right?

Meanwhile, the Viet Nam war was growing into a major international war. North Viet Nam was being supported by the Soviet Union with weapons and advisors. The U.S. had committed a total of over 485,000 troops in 1967.[4] Teenage boys and to a certain extent teenage girls were trying not to pay attention to all the numbers. The number of troops going in to the service, the number of troops killed in Viet Nam, the number of families grieving, the number of wounded.

My cousin Roger and friends Kenny Yager, Eddie Groves, and Ed Rohr had already gone, and so had many other classmates and acquaintances. My good friend and classmate since the fifth grade, Bill Stamm was starting his second year at the Air Force Academy. The point being, I knew the clock was ticking as far as my chances of being drafted as well. Playing music, having fun, spending as much time with "Ruby" as I possibly could, drinking beer as often as I could, couldn't change that fact. And then there was the fact that I was not paying enough attention to classes at OCC, and my grades were reflecting that.

Between my friend Blair and my friend Pat Stone, we found too many reasons to go party instead of attending classes. But, as I stated earlier, there didn't seem to be a good enough reason to really bear down and study a lot when, as many of us were aware, the military would be sending us greetings relatively soon.

Eddie Groves and Roger had gone into the Marine Corps together on the so called "buddy" plan. That simply meant that they would go to boot camp together and stay together during that period. That did not mean that they would go to Viet Nam together or have the same MOS (job). Eddie was assigned to the infantry. He was the classic Marine rifleman. He was deployed almost immediately after completing his advanced individual training (AIT) in infantry skills.

Unfortunately I don't have the date that Eddie arrived in Viet Nam. But as the Newton Press-Mentor reported—Eddie was wounded on September 6, 1967. The brief article simply stated that his injuries were to his chest, thigh and left big toe. The Groves family had received the information via telegram from the Marine Corps. They were told that his condition was good. So, at least in my circle of friends, the news that Eddie Groves had been wounded in Viet Nam brought the vicious reality of life and war right to our front door. And for those of us trying to just have fun, and ignore the war as best we could, it was a jolt. It was like a sucker punch to the gut. The ringing in our ears just got extremely loud.

Roger was sent to Camp Lejeune, N.C. for further training as a dispersing clerk. I felt good about the fact that Roger hadn't been assigned to an infantry unit, but I was aware that if you were on the ground in Viet Nam, you weren't in a safe place. Roger and I had talked about that when he came home on leave before he went to Camp Lejeune. It was just a matter of time until he would also be deployed to Viet Nam. Roger landed in Da Nang on December 1, 1967.

Approximately 10 miles to the west of Da Nang was the base camp for the 3rd Battalion, 5th Marines, 1st Marine Division. Eddie Groves' base camp. So the two Jasper County friends who joined the Marines on the "buddy" plan end up ten miles apart, 6800 miles from home. Weird things happen in life—and certainly in war.

Part Five

The Battles of the Bands

During the fall of 1967 both the Nite Raiders and the Illusions were quite busy. Both bands were playing regularly and building a solid fan base. Also during that period both bands were practicing even more than normal. The Nite Raiders were understandably not practicing in Yager's basement now, because Kenny was no longer in the band, so we practiced in various places, including the concession stand of the Fairview Drive-In Theater. The extensive rehearsals were to prepare for a "Battle of the Bands" at the Soybean Festival in Effingham on November 2nd.

There were to be nine bands from Effingham, Newton and the surrounding area in the "Battle." But we knew that the main competition more than likely would be our old friends, the Illusions. We weren't all that familiar with the other bands, but we couldn't take anything for granted either.

Of course winning a competition over other bands was always fun, but this time there was a special prize for the winners. Samuel Music Company had agreed to pay for six hours of recording time in a studio in Flora, IL. This was a very big deal for us, and for all the bands involved. The event was set for Thursday November 2nd in the basement of the Saint Anthony School. The pressure was on.

About a week before the contest I had come down with a severe cold, one of those that went immediately down to my chest. By Sunday night I was sick as a dog. I waited a couple of days, and with much urging from my parents, went in to see Doctor Hartrich. He listened to my lungs and had me cough a couple times, and determined that I had pneumonia in my left lung, and the right lung wasn't far behind. He gave me some pills and said that I needed to stay in bed for a few days. Well this was a bad situation because we were going to practice at least one more time before the "Battle", but that was not going to happen, at least as far as the drummer was concerned.

So I took the medication from Doc Hartrich, but still was running a pretty high temperature and each cough was painful. So that was all our "family doctor" needed to hear. My Aunt Fern had been to see her old friend Dallas Turner and bought one of his secret potions to apply to her patient—me. She came in with the jar of red liquid and some plastic wrap. I was lying on the couch so that I could watch TV between naps. Aunt Fern tells me to take off my pajama top, so she can apply the liquid to my chest, and wrap the plastic around it. I took one whiff of the red liquid and told her "no thanks." But Aunt Fern was very persistent in her need to apply this special potion, and get me well. So I finally gave in and let her apply the potion to my chest and let her apply the plastic around my chest. Besides the smell, the plastic wrap made it very uncomfortable and very hot. Dallas Turner was more popular for his calligraphy and his machine like writing, but as Aunt Fern explained to me, he also cooked up special potions for people in his cauldron, and they were really good.

I have no idea what was in the liquid, but Aunt Fern was sure that it would cure me. She came back the next day to re-apply the poultice. Between the medicine from Doc Hartrich and the special potion, I was starting to improve, but Thursday night was upon me. I still felt pretty rough, and I was beginning to smell like a piece of greasy fish.

I struggled to take a bath and load my drums, but I made a couple phone calls to assure the other band members that I would be there, no matter what. I had a pep talk with myself on the way to Effingham, trying to make myself believe that I actually felt better and to buck it up. This was such an important night for us. I certainly couldn't let the band down.

Jeff Crouse helped me carry my drums in, and wanted to know how I was doing. I told him I still felt like crap, but we would do just fine. It was going to be a long night. I certainly don't remember the lineup, as far as who went first etc., but I know that the Illusions went on before we did. They were very good. They looked great, and their songs went off without a mistake. I believe that each band was to play three or four songs.

I really don't remember if we were the last band to play, but we were right to be worried most about the Illusions. There were other good bands, but they were the main competition. So although I was nervous and felt horrible, we went on stage.

It was all over in about 15 minutes. We went through our mini set quickly and with no breaks between the songs. We just made a smooth transition from one song to the next, and the band was "tight." We all started together and we all finished together. When we finished our last song, I have to admit that we all felt good about our performance. During that few minutes on stage, I had forgotten all about having pneumonia, and feeling rotten. The adrenaline and the excitement of possibly getting the recording time had taken over.

Possibly there was one more band, it's hard to remember for sure, but shortly after we were finished, the judges took a short time to get their heads together and make their decision. It was nerve racking for a few minutes. Finally one of the judges went on stage with the results. He announced the runner up first. It was the Illusions.

I was standing near my good friends Mike Yager and Art Hunzinger when the announcement was made. The disappointment on their faces was hard to watch. The judge waited for a few seconds and then said "And ladies and gentlemen the winner of the Soybean Festival Battle of the Bands is.....The Nite Raiders."

Not only did the crowd start cheering, so did we. This was the biggest thing ever to happen to the band, and the recording time is something that we never thought we would be able to do. We also got a nice plaque to go with it. And although I felt bad for the Illusions, man we were all happy. And normally this would call for a few beers somewhere, but as soon as I got my drums packed up, I was headed for home. The remains of being sick were still hanging around. And in three weeks we would be in another "battle of the bands" in Robinson, but first some time to heal up.

The next three weeks were very busy. Not only was the band busy playing gigs on the weekends, but we had to get our act together—literally—for the "battle of the bands" on Thursday November, 23, 1967 (Thanksgiving Day). There were to be only four bands that night, but again we were worried about one specific band. Greg and Jeff had a good friend by the name of Lander Ballard that was a great guitar player and vocalist. Lander was the leader of a band called U.S. Males, based in Robinson. And this competition would not be judged by "judges", it would be judged by the crowd.

Greg and Jeff were from Robinson as well, but U.S. Males were very popular in the Robinson area. We had decided that if the songs we played in Effingham were good enough to win at the Soybean Festival, maybe we should stick with that set for Robinson. Again, we couldn't take the other bands for granted, even though we weren't that familiar with them. It was Lander and the U.S. Males that we were sweating about.

Through the luck of the draw, we were going to play last, so we had the entire evening to get more nervous. As expected, U.S. Males had a "kickass" set. Lander was on fire with his leads, and his rhythm section was very solid. We knew our concerns were valid. Our set was going to have to be flawless.

As we were setting up our equipment for our set, I noticed that some of our fans and followers from the Newton area were there, and to my surprise, my parents were there. They were always very supportive of my playing, but generally they didn't get to come to very many gigs. Even though we didn't talk about it before we took the stage, we all knew that again, our set would have to be flawless to have a chance against Lander's band.

Because there were fewer bands in this "battle" we got to play a couple more songs. Admittedly when we finished, I thought we had nailed it. I think we all felt good about the set. So now it was time for the crowd to cast their ballots. It took several minutes for that to happen.

I went over to hang out with my parents while the votes were counted, and of course they thought we had won. There could have been a bit of favoritism there, but I really appreciated it. So after about 30 minutes, the master of ceremonies went on stage to announce the winner. It went pretty quickly, and he announced the runner up was—U.S. Males, and the winner is—the Nite Raiders. Man we felt great. To beat another great band like Lander's band, after we had won against the Illusions just three weeks earlier was unbelievable.

The reason these "battles" were so important was because the news of a band winning them was like money in the bank. More places wanted you to play, and more people would show up to hear the band that won the "battle of the bands" wherever it may have been. We were very proud of our accomplishments. We were all good at what we did, but I truly believe what separated the Nite Raiders from so many other bands was Jeff Dalton. He played keyboards, he sang, and the real difference maker—he played a mean saxophone. He was very special.

The Nite Raiders were on a roll alright, and our schedule was filling up quickly. But we had to now get ready to go to the recording studio with enough material for at least two sides of a 45 rpm record. We knew we wanted to have an original on one side, and probably a cover on the B side. Quite frankly we had always been a cover band, always trying to stay on top of the top 40 hits and quality album songs. The band was practicing in the concession stand at the Fairview Drive-In at the time, during the week of course, we were still open on weekends in the winter. Our time schedule for recording was fast approaching. We had been informed that we had to be in the studio and done by about the middle of December, and we didn't have anything on paper as far as an original song so far.

Some of our favorite groups at the time were some of the Chicago based bands, The Buckinghams, The Cryan' Shames, and the New Colony Six and we were also fans of Paul Revere and the Raiders because of their saxophone parts. So with that in mind we started writing some lyrics. It actually went pretty smooth. Everyone was participating and giving input, so it was indeed a band effort.

When we agreed on the lyrics, of course the next step was to get the music track put together. Between Jeff Dalton, Greg Crouse and Elmer Zumbahlen, they put it to music pretty fast. Jeff Crouse (rhythm guitar) and I were waiting to see where we needed to go with the fill in. Once everything started to come together, the multiple playing and replaying began. The original was called "So Wrong" and it was beginning to sound pretty good. If my memory serves me correctly, we left the equipment set up in the concession stand and came back the next night to rehearse again. Also on the agenda was deciding what song to put on the B side. We decided on an instrumental version of the Paul Revere and the Raiders cover "You Can't Sit Down." That song was already on our set list, and we played it pretty much every night that we played. So the songs were set. We just had to set the date to record.

For whatever reason, the night to record was on a week night. We had never been in a recording studio before, and Ray, the owner, had never recorded a rock band before. He typically had been recording gospel groups, some with music behind them and some with just vocals, so it was going to be an interesting and challenging night for all of us.

The studio was upstairs, so first we had to lug our equipment up. By the time we got all our equipment in the room, Ray was already shaking his head. It was snug in there. I had to set up in a little cubicle with some sound proofing set around the drum kit. That was certainly a new experience. After we finally got all the mics hooked up and ran into the board, Ray told us to play something, just to check and see if everyone was coming through the board. Like I said, he wasn't used to hearing a rock band fire up and all that sound coming through his board. It took a while to get things in balance before we could attempt take one of "So Wrong." Also, none of us had ever played with headphones on, it felt really strange-- so we all had some things to get used to.

It took five takes for "So Wrong", but finally everyone agreed that it was well balanced and the vocals were strong enough. Then it was time to start on "You Can't Sit Down." Needless to say, Ray had never recorded a drum solo either. That was a pretty big part of the song. That song actually turned out to be harder to record and get balanced than our original song, but eventually we were all satisfied, or at least let it go.

So when we got all our equipment back down the stairs and got it loaded, we were all just sort of standing around with a smile on our face and saying, "Man do you believe this, we just made a record." Overall it was very cool. We, if memory serves me correctly, ordered 300 records. The idea of course was to play the songs on the record at our gigs, and sell them to our fans. We were proud of what we had accomplished. We could legitimately bill ourselves as recording artists. How cool is that.

The weekends were definitely filling up with gigs, and we were indeed able to ask more money than we used to. I remember the days when we used to play for $50.00 for three hours and all the fish we could eat. Those days were behind us and now most people realized we were worth more money. Things were definitely looking up for the Nite Raiders, but as far as relationships and school.....not so much.

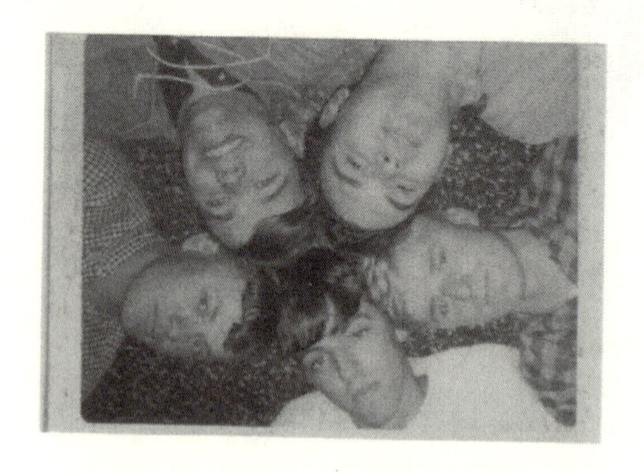

Nite Raiders Going to State Fair

1967

The Nite Raiders, a musical group of young men from Jasper county will appear at the Illinois State Fair Saturday, Aug. 12, in a talent contest or "battle of the bands."

Members of the group are Ken Yager, rhythm guitar, Ron Kinder, drums, Elmer Zumbahlen, bass guitar, Jeff Dalton, organ saxophone and singer, and Greg Crouse, lead guitar. Greg is from Robinson.

This will be the last time the band will appear together as Ken will be leaving to join the armed forces.

The band has had a lot of fun plus lots of hard work in the past year, playing in both Indiana and Illinois.

The Nite Raiders will play tonight at the Teen Tower in Oblong.

Local Bands Finish at Top of Contest

The Nite Raiders of Newton were first place winners in the Battle of the Bands held last Thursday evening at Effingham. The Illusions of Newton took second place among the nine bands participating.

Members of the Nite Raiders are Greg Crouse of Robinson, who plays lead guitar and helps with the vocalizing, Jeff Crouse, his brother, who plays rhythm guitar, Elmer Zumbahlen of Wheeler, playing the bass guitar, Ron Kinder of Newton on the drums, and Jeff Dalton of Newton, playing the organ, sax and doing the vocalizing.

As first place winners, the Nite Raiders received a plaque and the opportunity to make a recording under a Decca or Columbia label.

The Illusions, composed of Mike Yager, Art Hunzinger, Jim Logan and Larry Reich, finished only eight points back of the winners. According to Mike, the Illusions were rated tops in showmanship and appearance.

Top: Nite Raiders promo photo 1968

Bottom: Newton Press-Mentor articles about The Nite Raiders.

Top left: Ron Kinder original drum head

Top right: The Nite Raiders at Teen Tower-Oblong

Bottom: Ron Kinder celebrating after winning the battle of the bands in Robinson.

Part Six

A Cold Wind

During the winter of '67 and into '68, it was a typical Illinois winter. Cold and snowy and just plain unpleasant, but if you were playing music, you knew you had to just suck it up and go where ever you had to go. I remember one such night after playing in Marshall, IL. We followed the snow plow for as long as we could, to let him break the trail. It was certainly a slow trip home that night, but that's just the way it was, you did what you had to do.

And then later that winter, between Greg and Jeff and their dad John Crouse, they found a 1965 Corvair van for sale. It had been a delivery van for something in or near Robinson. It had only one seat, just for the driver. It also needed a transmission. I don't remember what it cost, probably just a few hundred dollars. John Crouse had agreed that we could park it in one of his repair sheds, so we could change out the transmission. John was in the oil well service business. So we had a place to work, and plenty of tools, it was the knowhow and experience in working on a Corvair van that we all lacked. Either John or Greg had found a used transmission somewhere and got it to the shop, which was just an uninsulated pole barn, with what I seem to remember had a dirt floor.

When we all gathered to start the job of changing out the transmission it was so cold in the building it was absolutely miserable. Our hands were so cold that you couldn't hang on to anything for very long. I don't remember exactly how many sessions we had or how long it took, but eventually we got the transmission in, and believe it or not, it worked. The engine ran pretty good for a Corvair.

So the band had "moved up" to a vehicle that would carry all our equipment and all the band members at the same time. The way the insurance worked though, Greg was supposed to be the only driver, and then there was the fact that there were no other seats in the van. We put a bean bag in the front seat area for someone, and the rest of the band had to find a place in the back somewhere amongst the equipment.

Now we didn't all travel in the van for every job. If the job was in Robinson or closer to Greg and Jeff, we would bring different vehicles. For most gigs, Greg would pick us up, and away we would go—all packed in there like sardines—but we still thought it was pretty cool.

I remember one specific night after a gig at a high school dance—naturally we were all hungry afterwards—there had been a lot of food there, along the back wall of the gym. So on the way out with equipment we were grabbing whatever was left, which was mostly pie—specifically cherry pies—yeah whole pies.

So after we got paid and hit the van, we were ready for some cherry pie, the problem was we hadn't thought about grabbing any forks or spoons, so we had no choice but to just use our hands. What a mess that was, but it was good. And the guys in the front were hollering to the back saying "hey how about passing some of that pie up here", so we just started passing whole pies to the front, and they were using their hands as well. We all had cherry pie all over our faces and hands, and I'm sure the equipment as well, but man it was fun. We were all laughing and stuffing pie in our mouths as fast as we could. Those are memories you just can't buy and certainly don't want to forget. Later in life when we were all together, we always had to relive that cherry pie story. It was great fun.

Also during that winter "Ruby" and I had broken up. She wanted freedom to be with other guys and have fun on her own. She said I was putting too much pressure on her as far as the getting married part. And she was probably right too. I finally came to realize that I was trying to possess her, and that is never a good thing. But before I came to understand that, I sort of went off the rails.

Blair and I and our good friend Alan Beard tried to take partying to a new level. All of a sudden I was back to the idea of there never being enough of whatever it was that we were consuming. Blair, Alan and I, along with many others were in constant party mode. I had started dating "Annie," who was actually younger than "Ruby."

School was certainly not a priority. Many of my classmates, friends and family members had already either been drafted or volunteered for service to our country. My personal goals and direction had suddenly gone into a dark place. I had taken a job with Jasper Wood Products in the quality control section. I didn't like the job at all. Blair was working at Norge (later Fedders) in Effingham, and he really didn't like that either. And even though the band was hitting on all cylinders, I was starting to think about the fact that I should be doing my part, as far as the service was concerned.

I was beginning to think about volunteering for the draft. Just go in the Army for two years and get it over with.

One night after a big snow in the winter of 1967/68, Blair and I had been drinking some beer at Alan Beard's house. I know there was one other person, but honestly I can't remember for sure who. We apparently were bored and needed something fun and exciting to do, so we piled in to Blair's old Chevy—the frog—and began driving around the regular cruise route, the square to Dulgar's Seed House, the Dog-n-Suds would have been closed during the winter, back to the square, down to Neese's station, back to the square, and then we decided to head out to the high school for something different.

When we got there the parking lot on the north side had been plowed, but it was still really slick, so we decided to start doing some figure eights and donuts. Everything was going great and we were all laughing like crazy, just having a blast, and then after one of the maneuvers, as Blair was trying to get control of the car again we ended up heading right towards the school. Blair slammed on the brakes, but it was so slick it did no good at all. We jumped the side walk and—BAM—we hit something solid and came to a stop. All the laughing stopped at that point too, and we all got out, to see what the heck we had hit.

Partially buried under the snow that had been plowed off was a base holding a large flood light, which was shining on the school, at least it was before we got there. Blair got back behind the wheel, and the rest of us pushed and tried to pick up the front end while the old Chevy spun the back tires like mad.

After several attempts and a lot of swearing, finally we got it backed off the broken light. We all realized that we needed to get the heck out of there as fast as we could. We slid and fishtailed our way back to the highway, and headed for Alan's house. We turned and went over to Washington Street and up to the square before heading south to get to Alan's house.

Just about the time we turned south, about a block behind us, the red lights of the city police car came on. We all assumed that it was Doc Jourdan. Someone must have called the police after seeing our activities at the high school. Instead of stopping, Blair just sped up and turned east towards Alan's. By the time we got in front of Alan's house Doc Jourdan was about a half a block behind us. We all bailed out of the car and started running through the knee deep snow towards the back of the house instead of all going in the front door. Like I said, we had been drinking some beer, and I guess it seemed like the right thing to do at the time.

We hoped that when Doc realized that there were several of us back there, that he wouldn't want to come around there by himself. Although if he had, he would have caught us all red handed, just standing there in the snow shivering. But he didn't come back there. He sat in the police car out front for about fifteen minutes, I'm sure checking on Blair's license plate etc. and finally drove away. Maybe he figured leaving us standing back there wandering what was going to happen next was pretty good punishment, I don't know, but I can assure you we didn't drive Blair's old Chevy around anymore that night. We stayed put, and just laughed about it.

It certainly could have been a lot worse for all of us, but that was one of the advantages of living in a small town when times were less complicated.

Not long after that I made the decision that, since I had flunked out of OCC, I really didn't like my job at Jasper Wood Products, and I was feeling guilty about still being in Newton having a good time while so many of my classmates, friends and family were already gone, some already in Viet Nam, that I would go down to the Selective Service office and talk to Mrs. Weber—the lady in charge of the draft board—and tell her to move my name to the top of the list to be drafted.

Mrs. Weber was a very kind lady. She talked to me about it, and asked me if I was sure that's what I wanted to do. I told her that I had given it quite a bit of thought, and yes that's what I wanted. She agreed to do it, and told me that I would be included in the next group to be called to take their physical in St. Louis. At least I had started the ball rolling. The ringing in my ears was starting to be a roar.

I had mentioned my thoughts to my parents. My dad was at least understanding about it. He and both his brothers had joined the Navy not long after Pearl Harbor. My mom on the other hand couldn't believe that I would do that. I also understood her feelings. She had lived with the anxiety and fear of my dad serving in the Sea Bee's in the south Pacific for three years, plus she knew a lot of the families who had sons in the service during the current Viet Nam war. And with the war being televised each night right in to the living room, the families of the service men and women went through their own little bit of hell each day.

Then sometime in March 1968 I received my notice to go to St. Louis and take my physical for Selective Service. I don't remember the exact date, but it was cold and we had to be at the Greyhound bus station in Effingham at some ungodly hour—probably 4:00 am. I seem to remember that either one or both of the Woods boys—Jerry and Jag—made the trip that day as well. The bus was full of young men from Jasper County wandering what the heck would happen when we got there.

When we got there we were herded into the facility, and first into large rooms that were like large classrooms. I seem to remember that we were timed as we filled out a large amount of paper work, including your medical history and what ailments that you might have. I remember some guys asking other guys across the aisle what things meant and what did you say, like it was a test for a grade or something.

Once the paperwork part was done we were told to follow the sergeant or whatever he was down to some lockers, where we were told to strip down to our underwear and put our clothes in the locker. Then the infamous words that anyone who has ever taken a military physical has heard “get in line single file and follow the yellow line”. Everyone heard that about a hundred times that day.

As you followed the yellow line you went to various stations where different doctors weighed you, took your vital signs, checked your eyes, and then there was the room where you were told to get in a large circle and when told, turn around , drop your shorts and spread your cheeks. Yeah...that was a little awkward in a room full of guys you didn’t know. The best for me though was the urine sample. The instructions went something like this—“Alright listen up, go to the table—pick up a cup—take the cup in to the bathroom—piss in the cup—bring the cup back to the table—give the cup to the doctor and go stand over there.” That may not be exactly the words, but its close. The best part though, was some guys couldn’t get a drop to come out, due to stage fright or whatever, and they would ask the guy next to them to give him some of his. Or guys were swapping their cups with other guys, I guess to confuse the system, and I swear I saw one guy bring back a cup of some kind of blue liquid. I have no idea where he got that. But I’m sure that the people there at the center had seen it all before. There’s nothing new under the sun so to speak. And just when I thought I was done, I was turning in my paperwork to the last group of doctors, one of them says “Kinder you have to go back and get another x-ray.” I thought, man I’m ready to get my clothes back on instead of going backwards in this line, but I didn’t have any choice in the matter.

I went back into the x-ray room and had to lie down on the cold table again for another x-ray of my back and chest. I asked why I had to come back for another x-ray, and the guy just said that the other one wasn’t clear enough, so they had to take another one. So I accepted that and went to get my clothes.

I also found out that cousin Jerry Woods had to go back for some further questions about a ticket that he had gotten for drinking and fighting as a teenager. They basically wanted to know if he had been rehabilitated. It was like the line from the movie “Alice’s Restaurant.” Arlo Guthrie’s character had been ticketed for littering in the movie, and when he went to take his army physical, they took him aside to ask him, “Boy have you been rehabilitated?”

So that was out of the way, and now it was just a matter of time until the next group would be drafted from Jasper County.

One thing that remained consistent during these rocky times was the fact that I still loved to hang out at the Yager home. It was my home away from home, so to speak. Mike and I had become even closer friends now that Kenny was in the service. And my parents were always glad to see Mike or Alan or Blair or Art or whoever I was hanging out with as well, but it was a different atmosphere at Yager's house.

One of my favorite examples is this. One night after Mike and I had been out somewhere and had returned to his house, we decided that the roof of the garage looked like a really good place to finish out the night and have another couple of beers. So either the ladder was already there or we got the ladder and climbed up to the peak of the roof and sat down. We were talking and laughing and finishing off a couple more beers and then when we were finished with the beer, we simply let the can roll off the roof and clang around on the concrete below. It was cheap fun, but we were enjoying it.

After we had been up there for thirty minutes or so, a car pulled up the driveway and into the garage. It was Ray, Mike's dad. He had closed the Royal Tavern for the night and was just getting home. He came out of the garage and headed for the back door when Mike hollered at him “hey dad”, Ray looked around for a second and then finally spotted us on the roof. He said “what are you guys doing up there?” Mike said “drinkin’ some beer, you want to come up and join us?” I actually thought that after a long day and night at the Royal Tavern, and being on his feet all day, that Ray would probably say “thanks anyway I’m going to bed”, but he didn’t. He climbed up and joined us on the peak of the garage. He opened a beer and sat there with us and shared stories and laughed right along with us. And when he was finished with his beer, he let the can roll off the roof and clang around on the concrete below too. Like I said, it was a different atmosphere at Yager’s house, but one I’ll never forget.

Part Seven

The Lightning Strikes

When there's a war going on and you know that the next time people from Jasper County are called, your name will be there, it's hard to get comfortable for very long at a time. The band was still playing a lot, I was dating "Annie" but it was definitely not going to be a long term thing. I was also beginning to be very interested in another young lady named "Brandi." And she was also a lot younger than me. I'm not sure why that trend got started, but that's what was going on. And of course I was still hoping for some reconciliation with "Ruby". It was beginning to be a little complicated.

So life was pretty normal as spring rolled on. I had also started having a few dates with a girl from Effingham, "Alice." The search continued for just the right one. I had a ton of friends to hang out with, Blair of course and my good friends Bruce Ward, Bob Klier and Rhondal McKinney when they were home from college on weekends or holidays. Bruce was attending the University of Missouri at Rolla, also known as the School of Mines. He was going to be a civil engineer. He was also singing in a rock and roll band.

Bob and Rhondal were both attending the U of I in Champaign-Urbana. Bob was going for a degree in aeronautical engineering I believe, with a special interest in propulsion systems. Rhondal was majoring in mathematics. Photography would come later. Plus he and Bob were roommates.

At one point I remember asking Bob to please find and buy the John Lennon and Yoko Ono album for me. It was the one in the brown paper cover and when you took off the brown cover there was a full frontal nude picture of John and Yoko. It certainly wasn't available in Newton, but Champaign-Urbana had a lot of stuff that you couldn't find in Newton.

So Bob finally found it and brought it to me one weekend. I thought, oh man this is going to be so cool, and no doubt it will be a collector's item. But when you took the cover off and revealed John and Yoko standing there naked.....it wasn't nearly as cool as I thought it was going to be. And the music on the record was definitely not exciting. In fact it was really bad in some cases. But Bob had done his job, and now I had the "collector's item" and a conversation piece that few, if any other guys had, in Newton anyway. Priorities change as we get older, and sometimes we look back and wonder "what in the world was I thinking?" and sometimes there's just no good answer.

Shortly after noon on April 19, 1968 I got a phone call from Mike Yager. His voice was somber and he went directly into his message for me. He said "Ron I've got some bad news, Kenny has been wounded". He really didn't need to say much more, and I couldn't even speak for a few seconds. When I did, all I could say was "so...how's he doing?" Actually Mike didn't have a lot more information either.

All the War Department told them initially was that he had been wounded in the right arm while on a combat mission. He had been treated and was in a hospital in Viet Nam. Other than that, the family just had to wait for more information to come through. When I hung up and told my parents what Mike had said, they were just sick about it as well. I had an immediate feeling of depression. I could barely make it into the couch to sit down. My parents came in and sat down and we went over the conversation again. And after a few minutes I realized what I needed to do—I had to go be with the family.

It was a very sad and yet a happy gathering. The sadness, of course, that Kenny and now the entire family was going through a very traumatic and anxious time was evident, but then there was a happy element in the conversations as well. The fact that Kenny was wounded but alive, and was being treated in a hospital was something to hang on to. All I could do was just be there.

It was a surreal situation to be there talking about Kenny being wounded. Of course we all knew it could happen. We all saw the news coming into our living room each evening. Eddie Groves had been the first friend to bring the reality of war up close and personal when he was wounded. But Kenny and I had been best friends, classmates, band mates and experienced new things together. This was different.

After I spent some time with the family, I realized that I needed to call the other members of the Nite Raiders and give them the bad news. This was going to be a tough one.

Within a few days Ray and Gertrude received a letter from Kenny to further explain his wound and the situation surrounding the combat mission. He told them that he indeed was wounded in his right arm and the bone was broken and also the muscle and the tendons were damaged. He told them that his arm had been put in a cast and the cast extended all the way down to his waist. He was due to be evacuated to Japan soon. He also told the family that he felt fortunate to escape with no more serious an injury because many of the men in his group were killed during the ambush.

When I heard that and then read the newspaper article about it, it was something that just stopped me in my tracks. It became very evident then that Kenny was not only fortunate, but that he had seen things that day that would never go away.

Someone else who was very helpful during that time was David Newton. David was the chairman of Service to Military Families for the Jasper County chapter of the American Red Cross. He personally delivered messages to the Yager family after Kenny's injury and gave them updates on when Kenny would be moved to a different hospital etc. And I'm sure David did the same for many other families, but I never knew about his help and compassion until Kenny was wounded. David was the manager/editor at the Newton Press Mentor.

At almost the exact time of Kenny's injury, Mrs. Elizabeth Housh of Newton received word that her son Specialist 6 Anthony Housh had been missing in action since April 19 (1968). There were no further details, he was just missing. Sgt. 1st Class Tony Housh was a flight engineer on a Chinook helicopter that was shot down while trying to deliver a 105 mm howitzer to a battle site.[9] As bad as it was for the Yager family and Kenny's friends and classmates to hear about Kenny's injury, at least we knew where he was, and where he was going. All Mrs. Housh, her family, and Tony's wife and small daughter could do was wait—just worry and wait.

The anxiety and worry and angst that families feel when loved ones are at war has been going on for centuries, but until each generation faces it head on, it just doesn't register in the reality bank of your brain, but when it does register you can never look at life and war quite the same. And I guess that's a good thing.

For whatever reason the Nite Raiders did not play on the weekend of May 3rd and 4th 1968. It was unusual to have the entire weekend off without playing. Friday night May 3rd was also Prom night for Newton Community High School and the Fairview Drive In was again having a movie just for the kids who had attended Prom. The movie was after the regular movie, so it usually wouldn't start until at least 11:00 o'clock, which meant the show wouldn't be over until about 1:00 am.

Since I wasn't playing that night I had agreed to help my dad at the box office. I worked it for the regular crowd and told him I would stay long enough to help get the Prom crowd in. The kids knew that they had to be there before the show started otherwise the entrance would be chained off. We also did that so that not just anyone could drive in for the late show.

After the box office closed I proceeded to go hang out with some of the people, in particular some of the girls that had come to the show without dates. I remember that eventually we left the Drive In and headed into town, although there wasn't a heck of a lot happening in Newton at that time of night. My memory of what we did next is a little hazy, but I know they took me back to the Drive In and dropped me off at the entrance and I walked in from there. The show was almost over, so it wasn't long before my parents came over to the house as well. By that time it was probably about 1:30 am. We talked for a little while and went to bed.

At around 7:00 am on Saturday morning the phone rang at our house. Unlike today, there was only one phone and it was located pretty much in the middle of the house. I heard it ring, but in the case of early morning phone calls at the drive-in, it was usually always someone wondering if there were any cars left parked on the grounds or did you see so and so last night, or what time was the show over etc.

My dad answered it, and I turned over to go back to sleep. Within a couple minutes my dad was at my door and simply said my name. I wearily turned over to see what he wanted. He sat down on the side of my bed—my dad had never came in and sat on my bed before—and I could tell that he didn't want to say whatever it was that he had to say. He said "Ron I'm afraid I have some very bad news. Monty was killed early this morning, on the motorcycle." I immediately said "no that can't be, the bike is out here in the shed." My dad said "well he must have been here and took it. That was Jim Flagg on the phone—Jan had asked him to call you." Jim Flagg was a funeral home owner and coroner at the time. Jan was Jan Hayes, Blair's mom.

After a few minutes, once the initial shock and disbelief wave had subsided a bit, I got up to ask my dad about the initial information that Jim Flagg had given him. I told him that I didn't even know how Blair could have been riding at night, because the bike didn't even have a headlight on it, or a tail light. That's when my dad told me that he was with Jack "Coon" Neidigh, and that Blair had apparently been following "Coon" using his taillight and headlight as a guide. For some unknown reason, Blair had lost control of his bike and went down. He slid into the old brick wall/guard rail on the river bridge, on route 130 just north of Newton. He died of severe head injuries.

I couldn't help but be a little angry on top of my sadness and shock. I just couldn't help it. Blair knew better than to try and ride that bike at night. We had gone to great lengths to strip the bike down to make it lighter and use it for climbing hills, riding out through fields or to jump the ramps at the drive-in. That's why the bike was in our shed. I had been having some fun with it, jumping ramps.

By 10:00 o'clock that morning people were calling me at home to ask if it was really true that Blair had been killed. They were hoping it was just a rumor. Unfortunately, I had to tell them all that it was no rumor, Blair was gone.

Now I had no choice but to go in and be with Jan. I had no idea what I was going to say, I just knew that I had to be there. And when I got there and walked in to the small mobile home that Jan and

Blair lived in, and saw the other people there with Jan, I knew I didn't really have to say anything. I just sat down beside Jan and held her hand and cried for a while. There would be plenty of time to talk later.

Within a three week period one of my best friends had been wounded in Viet Nam, and another of my best friends had been killed on a motorcycle that I had helped turn into a bike that was not street legal. It was a dark time. I was not in a good place. But this was one of those raw, hard lessons that reality teaches you. You have no choice but to keep going on with life, as difficult as that may be at times.

At the time of Blair's death I had still not heard from the Selective Service Office, as to when I could expect to go into the service. Then about ten days after Blair's funeral I went out to get the mail after I saw the rural carrier go by. There within the stack of mail was the letter I had been expecting. My parents were both over in the concession stand, and I took the stack of mail over there waiting to open my notice for all of us to see at the same time. I put the mail on the counter and told them what I had gotten. I opened my notice first, fully expecting that when I unfolded the letter it would say that I had successfully passed my physical and was classified 1A, qualified to go to the service at any time. Instead it had a 4F, not qualified physically to be in the military.

My dad didn't say anything. He just looked at me waiting to see what my reaction was. My mom asked me what that meant, and I said "it means I don't GET to go." Well she got a big smile on her face and said "well that's good isn't it? You don't HAVE to go." I did not have a big smile on my face, and I said "yeah mom that's what it means, I don't have to go, but I want to go." My dad still hadn't said anything. He knew what my feelings were. I felt that it was my duty and responsibility to go serve. I wasn't crazy about the idea of going to Viet Nam, but if that's what happened, I was ok with it. I couldn't believe that I didn't pass my physical. I mean, at that time the military was taking anyone that had a pulse, or as the old joke went, if they stuck a mirror under your nose and it fogged up, you were in.

I knew that I wasn't ready to give up yet. I don't recall how I found out that Doctor Hartrich had a copy of the x-ray of my back, but as soon as I found out, I made an appointment to go see him. Surely there had to be another option.

At about the same time that the Selective Service thing was going on, Jan, Blair's mom, had asked if I would go with her to visit her husband Don. She said he had a lot of questions about how Blair died and she would really appreciate it if I would go with her. Without hesitation I said that I would.

Don, as you may recall, was incarcerated at what was then called the Southern Illinois Penitentiary (Menard) in Chester, IL. I had never been to Chester IL and had certainly never been to a maximum security prison for any reason. However, I knew Jan needed the support at that time. I don't remember what day of the week it was, but we left early in the morning because it was a long haul to Chester from Newton. There was really no easy way to get there. Chester is about sixty miles south of St. Louis, right on the Mississippi river. I believe it took about three hours to get there. Long before we arrived Jan told me that we would be thoroughly checked and examined before we went to the visitation area. She was right. Besides a thorough pat down, they checked in our mouths and in our hair for any form of contraband. Jan had to explain who I was and why I was there with her.

We were led into the visitation area and almost as soon as we sat down, Don showed up on the other side of the glass. Admittedly, Don didn't look like the typical person you picture being locked up in a maximum security prison. He was well groomed, somewhat handsome, and spoke intelligently. After he and Jan had exchanged greetings and spoken for a little while, Don turned to me and started asking questions about Blair, or as he called him, son. Don was Blair's stepfather, but he kept referring to him as son. Eventually, after he had asked how Blair and I had become such good friends and how and when we met etc. he got down to asking me about how Blair had died. He wanted to know every detail.

Even though it was difficult to recount all the terrible details about Blair's death, I tried to satisfy him and make sure that Jan didn't have to go through every detail with him. Eventually he wanted to know who all was involved with the investigation, and if they were reliable, and if there was another vehicle involved?

I did my best to answer all his questions, but it had become evident to me that Don was looking for someone else to blame or someone else to hold responsible. It became a little uncomfortable, but as the visit time came to a close, he was grateful for my visit and for supporting Jan.

Another thing that Don said several times while we were there was "you know Ron, I don't deserve to be here, I shouldn't be in this place." I didn't have any idea what to say. Jan chimed in a couple times and said "that's right honey you don't deserve to be here." Having heard his background from both Blair and Jan previously, I knew that they didn't put you in a maximum security facility for your first bad check or theft offense.

It was a very eerie and almost surreal experience. The sights and sounds, the smell and the general atmosphere made me quickly realize that I didn't want to be there for any reason, including another visit with Don. I hoped that Jan never invited me to go again. Thankfully she didn't.

A few days later I had my appointment with Doctor Hartrich. He had the copy of the x-ray, and would explain it to me in understandable terms, why I ended up being 4F instead of 1A. He explained that I had a fused vertebra in my lower back and that my spine was crooked in that area as well. Admittedly, it didn't look good. Doctor Hartrich was a kind and gentle man, but he was also forthcoming and honest when it came to telling you what the facts were about whatever ailed you. He said "Ronnie, this is never going to get any better, in fact as you get older you will most likely have chronic back pain." I said "ok, well I know the Army won't take me, but maybe I could go to the Navy or Air Force." Doc Hartrich said "no Ronnie, no one that sees that x-ray is going to accept you in the service. I'm sorry."

There wasn't much left to say. I thanked Doc Hartrich for his explanation and for being honest about it, and headed for home. It was another disappointing day. It was also another lesson in the raw facts about life. As much as you may want something, it doesn't always work, no matter how bad you may have wanted it.

Apparently while my life was seemingly unraveling, there were things going on behind the scenes, so to speak, that I was unaware of. My Aunt Fern knew me about as well as anyone in the world. She knew that I had not been a little angel while getting through my teen years. She also knew the recent circumstances that had just happened within the last few months, including breaking up with "Ruby." I talked to her about things that I probably would never have told anyone else. Of course she also knew that (her daughter-my cousin) Jane Ann and I were very close and talked about life issues a lot. Aunt Fern and Jane Ann had apparently been on the phone about my situation more than I ever realized.

Jane Ann and her husband Tom Ackerman now lived in Portland Oregon. It had been an interesting road for them to end up in Portland. Tom had left a teaching and coaching job at Newton Grade School for a better paying job with Illinois Bell (Telephone Company) in Rockford, IL. While there, Tom was asked to help coordinate and provide logistics and special phone lines for the FBI, who were at the time working on a kidnapping case in Rockford. The FBI agents working that case were so impressed with Tom's skills and especially his memory skills that they told him he should consider taking the qualifying test for the Bureau.

After the kidnapping case was wrapped up, Tom took the exam and he absolutely blew it away. Even though he didn't have a law degree he almost aced it.[5] After a thorough background check, Tom was given the opportunity to go to Quantico Virginia for his initial training, both physical and academic. Jane Ann and their three children, Brad, Brett and Julie came back to Newton and stayed with Aunt Fern while Tom completed his training.

Tom's first field office assignment was Oklahoma City. My best memory is that they were there for only about a year, and in 1967 Tom was transferred to the Portland Oregon field office. Tom and Jane Ann and the three kids were living just outside

Portland in Beaverton. I'm not sure what month they arrived there, but after the calamitous several weeks that had happened in my life, Jane Ann called in mid May 1968 to see how I was doing. I think she probably had a pretty good idea what the situation was after conversations with Aunt Fern and probably others.

Before the conversation ended she said that I should come out to visit for a few days. I was a little shocked by that, but after I thought about it for a while, I decided to go. I had never flown before and I thought that would be exciting, plus I didn't have any reason now, that I had to stick around Jasper County, other than the band, and I knew I could work that out.

Before things got so crazy at airports, you could actually call the airline of your choice and ask them what flights they had to Portland, Oregon and how much it cost. That's what I did—I called the St. Louis airport and made a reservation on Eastern Airlines leaving St. Louis late afternoon on Sunday June 2nd. I asked my friend Alan Beard to take me to the airport. My dad was unable to do that because of having to be at the Drive-In for the show that night. I guess I had been to the airport once before with my dad, just to pick someone up, but I had never been to the ticket counter or dealt with waiting at the gate for flights. Neither Alan nor I was familiar with St. Louis, but we successfully made our way to the airport, and he dropped me at the front door. I made my way to the ticket counter and got my ticket, checked the suitcase that I had borrowed from my parents, and found my way to the gate.

I saw several people lined up at the counter handing their tickets to a young lady, so I assumed that was what I should do, and indeed it was. She stamped and stapled my ticket and assigned me a seat, and I was ready to go. It would be a non-stop flight on a Boeing 727-Whisper Jet. I couldn't believe that I was actually about to take off on a big jet headed to Portland. I sat on the aisle with a young girl, maybe 13, in the middle and her little brother, maybe 9 or 10 by the window. The power and thrust of the airplane was something I never could have imagined. For a nineteen year old kid that liked to go fast, it was quite a rush.

After we were up and leveled off, and I couldn't really tell how fast we were going, I started trying to talk to the young kids beside me. This was their first flight as well. The stewardess (they were still called stewardesses then) fed us, and offered us Cokes, etc. The flight was about three hours I believe, and as we got to within about an hour of

Portland, the girl and her little brother were talking back and forth and giggling at each other. I paid little attention to them.

All of a sudden it felt like the captain had slammed on the brakes and we weren't going nearly as fast. Shortly after that he came on the speakers and said we were starting to descend into Portland. That was another first for me. Then the two kids beside me were giggling even more and the girl was turning red in the face. The little brother leaned forward and wanted to ask me something, so I leaned down to be able to hear him. Now the girl is telling him to "shut up" and "no don't you dare." I didn't have a clue what was going on. All of a sudden the boy blurts out "she wants to know if she can kiss you?" Now I'm a little embarrassed. I met this young girl all of two and a half hours ago—talked to her for maybe thirty minutes total—and now this. So I said "well-uh-yeah I guess so" and I leaned over and let the girl give me a little peck on the cheek. She and her brother are now giggling again, and I put on my seatbelt to land in Portland. It would have been interesting to hear the young girl's side of the story when she met up with her little friends. What a first flight it had been.

Tom Ackerman was waiting for me right there at the gate. You could still do that in 1968. Then I went down to the baggage claim area for another one of my "firsts." The visit was officially on. I felt better already. Within about thirty minutes we arrived at Tom and Jane's house in Beaverton, and a whole new experience was about to begin.

Part Eight

Scattered Storms

At the peak, the U.S. had over 536,000 troops in Viet Nam.[6] Protests regarding the U.S. involvement in the war were starting to pop up in major cities and especially at major college campuses all over the country. On April 4, 1968, Dr. Martin Luther King was assassinated in Memphis, and the riots that followed were chaotic and very violent. The fires and violence and death that followed Dr. King's death were something that most of my generation had never witnessed. As for the war protests, most of those were organized and coordinated by campus groups such as The Students for a Democratic Society (SDS), Revolutionary Youth Movement, Weather Underground and others. Growing up in Jasper County and attending a small community college, my group of friends and I and acquaintances had no knowledge of how these groups worked or who was behind them.

Tom Ackerman was very familiar with these groups long before I showed up for a visit. But my visit was just to have a good time and not worry about the war or what was going on at home. Tom and Jane Ann were certainly doing their best to make it a fun visit. They told me about a party that they had planned for the coming weekend. It would be a hippy themed party and the FBI agents that Tom worked with and their wives would all be there.

The very idea that FBI agents, under the directorship of one J. Edgar Hoover, would dress up as hippies was hilarious. This was one of the "straightest", most reserved and regimented groups of men that you could imagine. So I was really looking forward to seeing how it was that they would portray themselves as hippies. But before that party could happen, there was another major event to take place.

I was awakened by Tom and Jane Ann talking in the hallway. I raised up enough to see that it was a serious conversation, so I got up as quietly as I could, so not to wake up any other kids in the room. I asked what was going on, and we stepped in to the living room. Tom had been up most of the night, because he got a call about 1:00 am that down in LA, Senator Robert Kennedy had been assassinated.

Senator Kennedy had just won another primary in his bid to become the Democrat candidate for president. He was shot as he was leaving the hotel where he had just given a victory speech. All the FBI offices and agents had been notified, although the suspect had been apprehended at the scene. This was my first hint as to how intense and non-stop being an FBI agent could be. But they had their good times as well and the hippy party was still on for Saturday night.

When the agents and their wives started showing up for the party, it was funny to see what the agents had done to make themselves look like "hippies." Some wore wigs, and most had painted on beards. All had on worn out jeans and some sort of sloppy shirt or sweatshirt. The wives were a little more convincing in their long skirts and tie dyed t-shirts etc. The party was going pretty well, although not a lot of alcohol was being consumed. Tom and Jane Ann didn't drink at all, and most everyone else was very conservative about it. I may have been the one drinking the most. Then out on the street there was a very loud BOOM, and the sounds of crunching metal and breaking glass were evident. Everyone jumped up to look out the front window at the same time. A driver had crashed into one of the agent's car (a new Mustang if I remember correctly) and was in the process of leaving the scene, although his car was in pretty bad shape as well.

Now five FBI agents dressed as "hippies" are headed out the door to give chase to the hit and run driver, who was trying to make his escape from the neighborhood. That scene alone was worth the price of admission. They had no reservations about chasing this guy dressed the way they were, plus they had the ability to contact the local police and let them know the situation.

They caught up to the guy within about four or five blocks, just as he was about to get back on a main road. They managed to pen him in so he couldn't move, and all the "hippies" jumped out, someone opened his door and at least a couple of them yelled "FBI."

Well now the drunken guy had a very puzzled look on his face and says "yeah right, who are you guys?" Again they said "we are the FBI now get out of the car." Fortunately within a few seconds the local police showed up. The officer told the guy that he sure chose the wrong hornet's nest to poke.

When the guys returned to the house, needless to say the party mood was gone. The agent's car that was crunched had to be taken away by a wrecker.

But to me it was an experience that I would never forget. This was certainly something that I could never have experienced in Jasper County.

The next week was equally exciting. I had never been to the west coast, and never had seen the Pacific Ocean. Although I don't remember the exact day, we packed up the kids in the big black 1964 Buick Electra 225 and headed for Cannon Beach. The old Buick was a real boat. We had three little kids, me and Tom and Jane Ann in it, and had room for a couple more. Cannon Beach is right on Hwy. 101, right on the coast. I had been swimming in the Atlantic Ocean on my first trip to Florida, with the Woods boys.

We went down on a spring break, and stayed and worked at Tropical Park Race Track, where the Woods boy's dad Leland (Ding) was racing a couple of their best standard bred horses. There were four of us on the trip, my cousins Jerry and Jag, their friend Jerry Zumbahlen and me. We actually stayed at the race track in a "tack room" with Ding.

The four country bumpkins found a fantastic beach, with bikini clad girls running all over the place. We saw Jerry Zumbahlen taking pictures, and naturally assumed that he was taking pictures of some of those girls...but no, he was taking pictures of sea gulls. When we found that out, we gave him all kinds of grief, but he says "hey I can take pictures of girls anywhere, but you can't see sea gulls in Illinois." Well he had a point, but we gave him no slack. And as you might imagine, we found a way to drink some beer as well. There's a lot more to that story, but I digress.

When we got to Cannon Beach, I made a mad dash for the ocean. I wanted to get in the water of the Pacific. I ran into the water, like you would normally do in Florida. I got about six feet in the water and realized that this was a different story. It felt like I had jumped in a cooler full of ice. I'm not sure what the temperature was, but it definitely was not for swimming. Never the less, it was a beautiful day at the beach, as long as you didn't go in the water. So my new experiences outside Jasper County continued to grow day by day.

The next few days Jane Ann and I hung out together doing standard things like taking the boys to school, going to some of the agent's homes, shopping and talking about things at home. Jane Ann had a way of getting me to talk about things that were troubling me. So I opened up to her about Blair, not getting to go to the military, "Ruby" and a couple other things. Jane Ann and her mom, Aunt Fern, were always able to get me to tell them things that I would probably never tell my parents or even some of my friends.

Next on the list of things to do was to go downtown Portland to see the new movie "The Graduate" with Dustin Hoffman and Katherine Ross. Although the first time Jane Ann and I went downtown, the line to get in stretched all the way down one block and around the corner and almost completely down that block. We took one look at that line and said "forget it." The next day we left much earlier to go downtown and made it into the line about half way down the block, and that was about forty-five minutes before the show was to start. Once that movie started, you could tell that it was destined to be a classic. It had all the elements—great actors, great story, great music, and the classic sports car, the Alfa Romeo Spider. The movie did a tremendous amount of business and did indeed go on to be one of the classics.

And then on Saturday morning, before I was to leave on Sunday, Tom tells Jane Ann that he wants to take me downtown to the lingerie show for lunch. Now being a typical red blooded American boy, this certainly got my attention, but I was admittedly having little trouble tying in lunch and lingerie.

Tom went on to tell me that it was at a restaurant downtown that catered to men on Saturdays and the place would be packed. And he was right. When we got to the restaurant there were no parking places in their lot, so Tom drove around the block a couple times and in frustration decided to park across the street at another little restaurant that had put up signs saying that these parking spaces were for their customers only, and all others would be towed. So as we were getting out of the car I said "hey Tom that sign says….." and Tom just said "oh we'll be back before they even notice." So away we go across the street to the lunch and lingerie show. The place was indeed packed, and we were lucky to find a seat.

There must have been a dozen young ladies that came out two or three at a time with different little skimpy outfits on, and they would walk around the tables smiling and suggesting that the outfit they had on would look great on your wife or girlfriend. We did order some lunch, but I must admit not a lot of guys were paying a lot of attention to their sandwich. The show went on for about forty five minutes and the young ladies were tipped well, however I don't remember seeing anyone buying lingerie. Tom and I finished our lunch and talked about how much we enjoyed seeing the latest in lingerie fashion and had some laughs. It was a great time. But all good things come to an end and we headed back to the car.

The parking lot of the restaurant where the show had been was clearing out, so we were dodging cars and eventually made it back across the street, only to find that the parking space where we left the black Buick Electra 225 was empty. Both of us stood there with our mouths open for a second, looked at other spaces, and then realized that the Buick had been towed. I didn't know what to think, having never had my car towed before, and Tom couldn't believe it either, so we stepped inside the little restaurant and the man at the counter says "hello—two for lunch?" Tom says rather sternly, "no I'm not here for lunch, I want to know who had my car towed." The guy says "well sir, we posted the signs so that people wouldn't park in our spaces and then go across the street to the other restaurant" (I don't remember the name of either place).

More words were exchanged, but the unfortunate fact was that we were now on foot. So Tom asked him what yard it was taken to, and the guy handed him a business card with the information on it. Tom was familiar with the impound lot. We didn't have any choice but to call a cab to take us to the lot.

We walked into the place and found the guy in the cage with the little window that was apparently made for little children to talk through, and the guy says “help you.” Tom says “yeah...I’m here to pick up a black Buick that probably just came in here a few minutes ago.” The guy says “black Electra 225 yeah it’s here, you wanna pick it up?” Tom says as calmly as he could, “yes...yes I want to pick it up.”

The guy asked for Tom’s driver’s license, and looked that over while he looked at some other paper work, and says “ok that’ll be thirty five bucks.” Tom sort of gasped and said “thirty five bucks—the car’s been here less than an hour, what do you mean thirty five bucks?” and the guy says “yep thirty five bucks—if it goes through that gate it’s thirty five bucks, doesn’t matter if it’s fifteen minutes or a whole day.” Tom was not a happy man. He was of course a little embarrassed about the whole thing, and really unhappy about the money to bail the car out. But we had no choice, so Tom paid the man and some guy from the back brought the car around, Tom signed for it and we were on our way home.

I totally understood Tom's frustration, but man to me it was just another great experience in a line of several others. I had to leave the next day, but I was so happy that Jane Ann had called and suggested a visit. It was more than I could have ever imagined.

I left Portland about noon on Sunday June 16th. My dad did come to pick me up that afternoon. He met me at the gate, and the first thing he said after he greeted me was "man I was sure glad to see that thing get on the ground." My dad had never flown and had no intention of ever flying. All the long distance traveling he had done during World War II was either aboard ship or on a train. He always said he couldn't believe airplanes ever got off the ground.

On the way home I told my dad about the new experiences and adventures that I had been exposed to. We laughed and talked about them all the way back to Newton. I could see that my dad was happy for me as well. I hadn't talked and laughed that much for several weeks. I guess that's what happens when young people get a little taste of what goes on in other parts of the country and the world. They realize there are a lot of things going on outside the "nest" so to speak.

I know now that my visit to Oregon in June 1968 was a game changer and life changing experience for me. I had come to a crossroad in my life, and I had to make a decision as to what direction I would take. Let's put it this way, I sat at the stop sign for quite a while before I decided which way to turn, but it wasn't an easy decision.

Part Nine

Heavy Clouds and a Little Sun

The Viet Nam war touched hundreds of thousands of families in the U.S. Jasper County Illinois was just a microcosm of the changes, the stress and the grief that went on in small and large towns all across the country. But for those of us in the small community of Jasper County, it was personal.

Almost everyone had a family member or friend or an acquaintance that had been drafted or had volunteered for service. The war that my generation tried to ignore during our high school years and even after graduation was now a daily reality check. It could not be ignored. It was a part of our daily lives and it wasn't going anywhere. The ringing in your ears was ever present.

Here's a list of some of my friends and classmates and acquaintances that answered the call. Some I have spoken with and have their permission to relate their stories in more detail. Some of the information gathered must be credited to the Newton Press-Mentor, with special help from the staff at the Newton Public Library. The list and stories are not meant to be in chronological order, they are meant to show the number of families affected by the war. It's evident that the troops suffered and many stories have been written about that, but there was also a lot of "silent suffering" going on within the families as well.

My cousin Roger and our friend Eddie Groves did indeed go to the Marine Corps together. Eddie was sent to Viet Nam ahead of Roger and was wounded at least twice. He received at least two purple hearts. While back in the states in July of 1968 Eddie still could not escape the effects of being in Viet Nam and was admitted to the hospital in Rantoul with malaria. Eddie was discharged from the Marine Corps on May 29, 1969.

My friend and classmate Ed Rohr enlisted in the Navy and graduated basic training in August 1967. Friend and classmate Terry Hampsten joined the Air Force and went to Lakland Air Force base in Texas for basic training. Friend and classmate Duane Pulliam enlisted in the Navy and was assigned to a Navy river patrol boat on the MaKong River as of July 20, 1967. He was wounded as well, although I don't have the date.

My lifelong friend and classmate Bruce Ward enlisted in the Army and left for basic training at Ft. Leonard Wood on August 27, 1968. Also 1965

N.C.H.S graduate and friend Rex Tarr left the same day. After basic training Bruce went to Ft. Knox for AIT in radio school. He then went to Ft. Gordon GA. for further training and was assigned to the 11th Armored Cavalry Regiment. Bruce arrived in Viet Nam on March 16, 1969.

Bruce was with an Armored Cavalry Assault Vehicle unit. Their unit saw a lot of action, and Bruce lost two friends in combat. His friend Smitty was killed in a rocket attack, and his friend Johnny Jones was killed in an artillery attack. Bruce's comments to me were that both deaths were just so "random." It just happened so fast and unexpectedly. They were just two guys in the wrong place at the wrong time. Bruce was not wounded, but the memories never go away. Bruce was discharged two weeks early at Ft. Dix New Jersey on March 30, 1970.

Kenny Yager's journey to Viet Nam started as many thousand other soldiers would start, in Fort Leonard Wood, MO. After eight weeks there, he was sent to Ft. Polk LA in mid-October, for his AIT (Advanced Individual Training) and in Kenny's case it was for further infantry training. Kenny said that about 95% of the soldiers that were sent to Ft. Polk were going to be deployed to Viet Nam. The timing was such that when he got his leave, he was able to come home for Christmas. So he at least had a holiday with his family and friends before heading to Ft. Lewis Washington to be staged and wait to be deployed to Viet Nam.

Kenny was aware that my cousin Jane Ann and her husband Tom Ackerman were living in Portland, Oregon, and through conversations with me and other family members Tom and Jane Ann knew that Kenny was going to be in Ft. Lewis. Arrangements were made for Kenny to take the bus down to Portland, and Tom would pick Kenny up downtown and take him to Beaverton for a nice home cooked meal and a nice long visit.

Whether Tom was running late or the bus was a little early, no one remembers, but since Tom was not there when Kenny arrived, he decided to walk down the street to the nearest bar he could find and have a couple cold beers until Tom arrived. This of course was decades before cell phones. Kenny found a bar within a couple blocks of the bus station and wandered in. Kenny said it was really dark in the bar, and it took a while for his eyes to adjust. After he got his beer and was about half way through it he noticed that there were no women in the bar, and a couple of guys were dancing with each other. And before he could gulp down his beer and get the heck out of there, a guy comes up beside him and offered to buy him another. Kenny told him "no thanks I have to go meet someone" which was really the case, but the guy followed him out of the bar and said "I'm sorry you have to go, but if you need a place to stay I can help with that." Kenny hot-footed it back to the bus station—met up with Tom—and headed for a much better situation.

The visit was really good, and Kenny got some good food, some good conversation, and was able to relax at least for one night. Tom took Kenny back to the bus station the next day for his three hour ride back to Ft. Lewis. As you can imagine that story was a source of good laughs with his Army buddies, as well as his friends back home.

Kenny landed in Saigon on February 6, 1968. That was also his dad Ray's birthday, and his grandma Yager's birthday. He told me that he was totally gung ho when he got there. In his mind at the time, he felt like he was ready to win the war on his own. He immediately volunteered to man an M-60 machine gun on a troop truck. The first night in Viet Nam wasn't bad. He even had a few beers with his buddies. The second night the Viet Cong blew up their ammo dump. Kenny said there were explosions going off everywhere, pieces and parts of the camp flying everywhere. He dove into a ditch, and was lying there with no ammo, and thinking that this was it. He was going to die the second night in country.

Kenny was assigned to the 199th Light Weapons Infantry Brigade. The key here is "light weapons." They could be picked up and transported to a different part of the war in a short time, because they didn't have to move a lot of heavy weapons or equipment.

They were a special bunch, and other infantry units were always glad to see them when they were brought in. Kenny's unit had been moved to an area of fighting near the border with Cambodia. They were on a patrol sweep, deep in the jungle on Thursday, April 18, 1968. The North Vietnamese Army waited until the patrol was within about 10 yards before they opened fire. Many soldiers were mowed down immediately.

Kenny was the assistant to the M-60 machine gunner. He carried much of the ammo. Both bandoleer's and boxes. Kenny probably weighed 140 pounds soaking wet and was carrying more ammo than anyone else in the unit. The machine gunner was wounded very quickly, so Kenny grabbed the M-60 and was ready to start firing when he was wounded in his right arm. He was hit between the shoulder and elbow. Bone, muscle, and tendons were all damaged. Airstrikes were called in and Kenny said the planes were firing rockets so close to them that it was unbelievable. Artillery came in as well. The sound, the heat and the explosions were almost right on top of them.

The lieutenant in command, according to Kenny, wanted to pull back. Kenny argued that they couldn't do that because there were still too many guys left out there. As with many veterans of many wars, there is only so much that they want to talk about, and we ended our conversation there. Kenny received a purple heart and a Bronze Star with a V for valor, for his actions that day.

He spent a few weeks in an Army field hospital before being moved to Japan for further care. Eventually, in late May he was moved to Ft. Riley KS for more surgery and rehabilitation.

My cousin Roger stayed where he landed on December 1, 1967, at the huge sprawling air base at Da Nang. The base was home to three different branches of U.S. troops, Army, Air Force and Marines. The Marines were the first to arrive there in 1965 and had been helping to defend the base ever sense. Because the base was so strategically vital to U. S. troops, it was under regular assault from the VC and NVA, typically by rocket or artillery fire.

Roger was a dispersing clerk for his unit, but that didn't mean he was nice and safe inside a building all the time. All Marines are trained to fight, no matter what their MOS (job) may be. Roger went on patrols around the base as well as pulling guard duty on many occasions.

He had pulled guard duty one night and had told his good friend and Navy corpsman Johnny Bomburger that if he didn't have anything else going on, he should come down to see him and shoot the bull. After Roger had been on duty for a while, sure enough his good friend showed up for some conversation and just to hang out with Roger. Shortly after that, a sniper shot Johnny Bombuger right between the eyes. He was killed instantly, not three feet from Roger. Roger was not wounded that night, at least not physically. When Roger and I talk about his experiences in Viet Nam and he shows me the pictures of his friend Johnny, I can tell that it's like it happened yesterday. Roger left Viet Nam December 11, 1968.

The battle for Hill 875, overlooking Dak To in the central highlands of Viet Nam is historically one of the bloodiest and most costly battles of the war in

Viet Nam. It involved companies and units of the 173rd Airborne Brigade—the 4th Infantry—the 1st-2nd-3rd-4th divisions of the 503rd Airborne Infantry Regiment and the 1st and 3rd divisions of the 8th Infantry. Many divisions of the ARVN (South Viet Nam Army) were also involved in the operation. By the time the fighting was over U.S. casualties totaled 361 dead—15 missing in action—1441 wounded. The fighting ended on November 23, 1967 after five days of battle for Hill 875. The entire operation for all the hills around Dak To had begun on or about October 3rd[7].

Also 40 helicopters were lost as well as 2 C130 Hercules transport planes and 1 F-4F fighter jet.

Unbeknownst to most of the people in Jasper County was that a 1965 N.C.H.S. graduate and Jasper County native was in the middle of the fighting for Hill 875. Ronald Delwin Granby, better known to us then as Delwin, was with Co. A of the 4th Medical Battalion, which was part of the 4th Infantry Division.

Mr. and Mrs. Granby knew their son was near the fighting for Hill 875, so when their son called them to let them know that he was ok, and back in camp—needless to say they were thankful and relieved.

Earlier I had mentioned the "silent suffering" that went on within the families of service members, and I believe that Mrs. Granby's words in an interview she gave to the Newton Press-Mentor convey the feelings and thoughts of thousands of families at that time.

Mrs. Granby said: "You watch the news on TV because you are afraid not to. Yet it makes your heart sick when you see what is going on and know your son is there." "You wait and you pray, for there is nothing else to do. You are afraid every time the phone rings. When someone knocks on your door you wonder if it will be something about your son. You watch for the mail each day, and when there are no letters you ask God once more to give you strength to wait another day."

"The phone rings, you are shaking all over when the operator says it is a call from Viet Nam. Then you hear that precious voice say, "Hello mom, what are you doing?" You thank God for letting you hear your son's voice once more. You ask Him to be with all the mothers who won't hear their son's voice again."[8]

T

op left: Roger Kinder & Ed Groves in Da Nang, Feb 1968

Top right: Bruce Ward in Viet Nam, June 1969

Bottom left: Kenny Yager in Viet Nam, April 1968

Bottom right: Roger Kinder & Ed Groves, Ed's base camp, Feb 1968

Most of the young men and young women that found themselves caught up in the war were innocently going about their lives just months before. Most guys were trying to figure out if they would have enough money to buy some beer after payday, or they were trying to talk some girl into getting into the back seat at the Fairview Drive-In.

Young ladies were trying to figure out how a young man with only two arms can all of a sudden be like an octopus, or did they have the right dress for the right occasion. Parents were just wondering if their teenagers were driving safely and will they be home on time. But as it has for many generations, war changes almost everything one way or the other. It changes how you think, what you feel, and for those directly involved—wondering if you'll survive.

In the meantime, the family of Spec.6 (Sgt. 1st Class) Tony Housh could do nothing but wait, speculate, worry and like Mrs. Granby, fear the phone call that may come from Viet Nam. At the end of the war Tony Housh and his crew chief Mike Wallace were still considered Missing in Action.[9]

Reality is a cruel mistress. It's always there, but sometimes it's very painful to accept.

Groves Injured in Viet Nam

Mr. and Mrs. Victor Groves of Route 1, Willow Hill, received a telegram today informing them that their son, Pfc. Edward Lee Groves, was injured Sept. 6 in the vicinity of Quang Pin in the Republic of South Viet Nam.

Injuries were to his chest, thigh and left big toe, received from an explosive device while on an operation. He received first aid treatment at the First Medical battalion and his condition was listed as good.

His address is: Pfc. Edward Lee Groves, [illegible], I Co., 3rd Bn., 5th Marines, First [illegible], 1st Marine Div., FPO San Francisco, Cal. 96602.

Kenneth Yager Is Wounded in Viet Nam

Word was received Friday morning by Mr. and Mrs. Ray Yager of Route 5, Newton, from the War Department, Washington, D. C., informing them that their son Pfc. Kenneth L. Yager, was wounded in Viet Nam on April 18.

A graduate of N.C.H.S. with the Class of 1966, the serviceman had been in Viet Nam since early this year.

His injuries, as reported by the War Department, include a gunshot wound to the right arm received while on a combat operation. He was treated and hospitalized in Viet Nam.

Dave Newton, chairman of the Jasper county Red Cross chapter's Service to Military Families, is awaiting word from the RC field director at the evacuation hospital after sending a message of inquiry through the Washington office to learn further details for the Yagers' concerning their son's condition.

In the meantime, the young serviceman is sure to welcome mail from home. His present address is: Pfc. Kenneth L. Yager, US 56568242, Hospital Mail Section, APO San Francisco 96381.

Yager Writes of Injuries

In a letter written April 19 from a hospital bed in Viet Nam, Pfc. Kenneth Yager tells his parents, Mr. and Mrs. Ray Yager, and family of Route 5, of the injury he received the day before while in combat.

The serviceman confirmed the earlier notification by the War Department, stating he received an arm fracture as the result of gunfire, and said that the muscles and tendons in the arm were also injured, and that a cast had been applied to the arm and extending to his waist. He expected to be evacuated by plane to a hospital in Japan on Saturday.

Kenneth told his parents that he considered himself fortunate to have escaped with no more serious injury because many of the men in his group lost their lives in the combat action in which they were engaged.

In a second message from Viet Nam, David H. Newton, chairman of Service to Military Families, Jasper county chapter, American Red Cross, received the following information regarding Pfc. Yager:

"Serviceman was transferred Monday, April 22, to 7th Field Hospital, APO San Francisco 96244 due to gunshot wound in right arm which fractured the humerus. Condition satisfactory. Prognosis not determined at this time. Serviceman will be hospitalized there six more weeks before medical evacuation to U. S. hospital closest to home for further treatment and convalescence."

Mr. Newton personally delivered the message to Mr. and Mrs. Yager.

Mail will be received by the serviceman addressed to Pfc. Kenneth L. Yager, US 56568842, 7th Field Hospital, APO San Francisco 96244.

Mrs. Housh's Son Missing in Viet Nam

Mrs. Elizabeth Housh of 429 East Decatur street, Newton, received a telegram Tuesday from Adj. Gen. Kenneth G. Wickham notifying her that her son, Specialist 6 Anthony F. Housh, 21, has been missing in action since April 19.

No further details were disclosed.

Specialist Housh had been serving for the past eight months with the U. S. Army in Viet Nam.

His wife, Marilyn, and daughter, Sherri Dee, 8 months old, live at Herrick.

The serviceman has a brother, Charles, 20, serving in the U. S. Navy, presently touring Africa and Europe. Two sisters, Mrs. Nancy Cooper and Miss Mary Housh, reside at 435 Burton street in Newton, and a married brother, Joe, lives in Decatur.

Buddy Gowin Is Killed in Viet Nam

Harry Dale (Buddy) Gowin, 20, son of Mr. and Mrs. Vonley Elmore of Route 2, Wheeler, has become the first actual resident of Jasper county to lose his life in the Viet Nam war.

Articles from The Newton Press-Mentor

Part Ten

Unpredicted Storms

By the summer of 1968 the world was moving pretty fast for me and my friends, and bandmates. Besides the constant news of the war, on major college campuses, protests of the war and those who were pulling the strings within the government and the pentagon were becoming more numerous and in some cases violent.

The Nite Raiders and the Illusions were both playing a lot. And for me anyway, playing, partying, and dating, was my lifestyle for the most part. I was working for my parents at the Fairview Drive-In and still getting to live at home, so I had a pretty good existence going on for a 19 year old about to turn 20.

By late May of '68, Kenny had been sent back to the U.S and was in Fort Riley KS for more surgery and rehabilitation. Knowing he was down there and at least beginning to recover was comforting.

At least we all knew that he was safe and not being shot at anymore. I still felt bad that I never got to serve, but I was beginning to accept the reality that it was never going to happen. And frankly after conversations with both Ed Groves and Kenny, on separate occasion, while tossing back a few beers, anytime I would mention that I felt bad about not going to Viet Nam, both of them told me almost the same thing. They said "are you serious, don't feel bad about that—hell everybody over there wants to be here. You were in the right place, don't worry about it man." That definitely helped my attitude. Two guys who had been wounded and made it home telling me that really helped.

By mid-summer the Nite Raiders had found a new place to rehearse. Jeff Dalton's brother Kent had purchased a place in the country that had a nice barn and an old house. Kent had a couple of thoroughbred horses and needed a place for them. The old house was not in great shape, but it had electricity, and the old living room had room enough for us to set up and practice. Ironically I had been in the old house on several occasions before it fell in to disrepair. It used to be where my friend and classmate Rhondal McKinney lived. Also ironic was the fact that Rhondal was one of the original members of the Nite Raiders. Strange but true.

By mid-July The Nite Raiders had been invited to play in a "battle of the bands" on Sunday September 15 for a big kick off to the 1968/69 school year. It would be held at The Spot teen center. We had seen some pretty stiff competition in "battles" before and had been lucky enough to be victorious on at least two occasions, but when the list came out for this particular one, we were especially concerned. There would be eight bands: The Fair, Fresh Clove Blues, Paper Sun from Charleston—Curiosity Shoppe—Effingham, New Spyders—from Indiana and The Nite Raiders—The Illusions—and Thee Livin Eynd from Newton. The judges were chosen from towns around the area to assure there was no partiality.

The Curiosity Shoppe was an outstanding band, and of course our old friends the Illusions were always going to be tough. They had developed a great show. The rest of the bands were lesser known, but you could never take any of them for granted.

By August 1st we had started learning some new songs for our set. One for sure was "Hello I Love You" by the Doors. I frankly don't remember the rest of the songs in the set, but I remember going over that song numerous times. Between playing the weekends and practicing a couple nights a week, we were staying very tight and things were coming together well for our show for the "battle".

We were scheduled to rehearse on, I think a Wednesday night around mid-August, and late that afternoon I got a call from Jeff Crouse, Greg's brother and our rhythm guitar player. Jeff said "we're scheduled to practice tonight right?" and I said "yeah that's the plan" and Jeff says "well I guess we'll have to practice without Greg." I said "why-where is he" and Jeff says "he went to Texas." I said "well when's he coming back?" and Jeff says "well I don't know Ron, it may be a while. He went down there to visit with some of our relatives, and he said he wasn't sure how long he'd be down there."

My temper got the best of me at that point, and I unfortunately took it out on Jeff. I said "he knows we're practicing for the "battle of the bands" right?" "What in the hell is he thinking? What are we supposed to do? Find another guitar player now?" Jeff said "well you know how Greg is; if he decides to go he just goes."

We all took our music seriously and having to pull out of a "battle of the bands" was something no one wanted to do, especially when you had a chance to go head to head with some very talented bands. But Jeff was right, Greg was as independent as they come, and if he decided to leave just on a whim, he didn't apologize to anyone for it, it was just his way.

The rest of the band was really bummed out as well, but we certainly didn't have time to audition a new lead guitar player, and go through the set list and put all the practice in for the "battle" show all over again. If I could have gotten my hands on my good friend Greg at the time, I probably would have done something I would have been sorry for. So all of a sudden The Nite Raiders were dead in the water. All the excitement and anticipation was quashed.

As timing, and I suppose some luck would have it, my cousin Jane Ann had let the family know that Tom had been offered the Special Agent in Charge position in Eugene, Oregon and they were going to be moving down there very shortly. Eugene is where the University of Oregon is located, and by 1968 it was quickly becoming one of the most radical campuses in the country. And at 28 years old to become the SAIC in a city like Eugene meant that the FBI must have had a lot of confidence in Tom Ackerman.

Admittedly at the time I didn't know anything about Eugene, OR other than it was south of Portland and had a big university.

I mention the timing because the band was essentially breaking up, Blair's death was still very painful, and I couldn't seem to get things going again with "Ruby", although I was dating a couple other girls at the time, and I still didn't have a firm direction to go with my life. Once again Jane Ann called to talk to me personally about the fact that they were moving down to Eugene.

Jane Ann was not the type of person to beat around the bush when she had something to say, so during that phone call she says "hey Ron you enjoyed your time in Portland didn't you?" and I said "well of course I did, it was a blast."

And once again, sort of out of nowhere Jane Ann says "well why don't you just come out and stay with us for a while and see how you like it out here, in Eugene." I was actually speechless for a few seconds, and finally I said "you mean actually come out and live with you guys and stay at your house and actually live there?" Admittedly I was stammering at that point. And Jane Ann says "yeah just live with us for a while. What do you have going on there that would keep you from it?"

At that point I knew that the lines of communication between my parents, my aunt Fern, and Jane Ann had been buzzing without my knowledge. Jane Ann had just enough information about my situation to know that I didn't really have anything that would keep me from going out there. She apparently knew that my life style was a little crazy and that I had gone off the rails a few times recently.

Truthfully once I had a chance to think about it for a while, I thought "what the hell" Jane Ann is right. What do I have to lose by going out there for a while. The next step would be to get my parents to sign off on the deal. I was old enough to make my own decisions, but I was helping dad at the Drive-In, and it was summertime, so we were busy.

My mom was not that happy about it, but at least I wasn't leaving for the Army. And I think looking back on it my parents knew that I probably needed a change in scenery, just to get out of the atmosphere that I was in and try something different for a while. So the decision was made. I was going to move west. I didn't know how long I would be there, and I didn't have any idea what I would do for a job, and the only people I knew were the Ackerman family, but I was going.

Now came the process of telling my friends and a couple of girlfriends that I was moving to Oregon. I had to tell the other band members that if they were going to try to move on without Greg, that they also would have to get a new drummer. That was a tough one, because getting to play with the Nite Raiders, and all we had been through as a group and as friends, made it all the more difficult to say good bye.

Besides my own family, my cousin and blood brother Roger, aunts, uncles, and grandparents, there was no other family that I was closer to than the Yager family. So going over to tell Ray and Gertrude and Mike that I was leaving for Oregon and didn't know when I might be coming back was almost more difficult than telling my own parents. Mike and I had become especially close after Kenny left for the Army and with the band and music connection that we had, he was almost like a little brother to me. It didn't mean that we wouldn't stay in touch, but it was going to be different for a while. That was a tough one.

Part Eleven

A Break in the Clouds

Wednesday, August, 28, 1968 was a pivotal moment for me. My dad walked with me all the way to the gate, and we stood at the window watching planes taxi in and out. I was excited and yet a little sad to be leaving my family and friends as I left for my new adventure in Oregon. My dad was nervous that day. Not only was I leaving home for an extended period of time, for the first time, but he hated to see me leaving on an airplane. He had a real problem with airplanes, and always said he never understood how they even get off the ground.

When it was time to board the plane, we shook hands and my dad wished me good luck, and said to be careful out there, and let mom and me know what's going on out there. I told him that I would do that, and that was it. There were no hugs. Neither my dad or I were "huggers." It just wasn't something my family did. There was no "I love you," another thing that my family just didn't do very much.

So I walked down the gangway to the plane, my head spinning a bit. The plane was another Eastern Airlines 727 Whisper Jet, just like my first flight to Portland. My flight went to Portland first, and then a little jump on a "wing flapper" down to Eugene. Tom picked me up at the Eugene airport and we took the short drive to my new home in Santa Clara, OR just outside Eugene. It was slowly starting to sink into me that I was about to move in and live in a house with my cousin Jane Ann, three kids, and an FBI agent. But I guess if you're going to make a change, it might as well be a big one.

Tom and Jane Ann wasted no time in introducing me to new people. That night, the neighbors from across the street, Jack and Joan Douglas came over to introduce themselves. Jack was a former Marine and had a barber shop in Eugene. Joan was a meter maid for the City of Eugene. There will be much more about Jack and Joan later in this writing. But that night we had some laughs, and Jack and Joan wanted to know more about my life and what I had been up to, so I started to feel more comfortable in my new home right away.

The day I left for Oregon, August 28, 1968 was also a pivotal moment for the country. The Democratic convention was underway in Chicago, and had turned very violent. The Chicago police department had been given the green light by the mayor, Richard J. Daley to put down the war protesters, whatever it took. Of course the coverage of the convention and the ensuing violence and chaos was interspersed with the coverage of the war itself, and it all came into your living room in living color each evening.

As far as the Democratic convention violence, I didn't know anything about the major players within the demonstrators and organizers of the entire thing, but Tom did. He knew who they were because he had been dealing with them either directly or indirectly ever since he had gotten assigned to the Eugene office. The University of Oregon campus in Eugene was a hot bed of all the major players who were protesting the war and the politicians who supported the strategy of how to defeat the communists in Southeast Asia. There will be a lot more to come about campus activities a little later.

Meanwhile, I was trying to get settled into my new home, and Tom, Jane Ann, and the three kids were trying to get used to me being there—in their house—as a permanent guest.

It actually went pretty smoothly. It wasn't like we were all strangers. The house was a split level with a full bath upstairs as were all three bedrooms, and a half bath downstairs. So as large families do on a regular basis, we made it work. Sometimes it was a little chaotic, depending on how many people needed to take a bath or use the restroom, but like I said, we made it work. For me though the biggest adjustment was the fact that I didn't have my own car. I had not given any serious thought to driving the approximately 2300 miles to Eugene from Newton by myself. The '63 super sport would just have to sit for a while until I decided where my life was headed. I knew my dad would drive it from time to time. In fact he liked to drive it to town once in a while.

One afternoon while I was working at the drive-in he asked if he could drive it town for a couple of errands, and I said "sure go ahead." He backed it out and told my mom to get in, that this was their ride to town.

So my parents do their errands, driving very slowly around town, and then head back toward the drive-in, my dad I'm sure, driving the speed limit, making sure my mom didn't have any reason to shout at him. But dad said as they were going across the bottoms past the river bridge my mom says "Well honestly I don't see what the big deal is about this car." "It's a nice car, but I don't see what the big deal is."

My dad just smiled and drove on slowly, past Yager's house and just past the road for the Jasper Lake and the new Saint Peter's Cemetery and then he came to a complete stop and said "you want to know what this car's got?" My mom says "well what are you doing-you can't just stop in the middle of the road."

With that my dad shoved it in first gear, cranked up some rpm's and let out the clutch winding it up in first gear—"Lamar" second gear, winding it up—"Lamar what are you doing?" third gear, cranking it up—"LAMAR YOU SLOW THIS CAR DOWN RIGHT THIS INSTANT." Fourth gear, just about the time they crest the hill to head down in the bottoms, about 110 miles an hour—"LAMAR ARE YOU TRYING TO GET US KILLED?" my dad with a big smile on his face lets off the gas and starts to slow down. He says "so what do you think of it now?" My mom says "if you knew how dangerous this car was, you should have never let him buy it, that's what I think!" My mom never rode in the Chevy again. My dad told the story and laughed about it for years, but I don't think my mom ever thought it was funny. But I sure did, and I still get a kick out of it to this day.

Tom and Jane Ann were very good about letting me borrow their family car, the big black Buick Electra. Man that thing was a boat, but really nice. We all knew that if I was going to be staying there permanently, I had to find a job, so many days I would make a list of places to check out and take off for Eugene in the Buick. In those days about the best you could do, if you didn't know someone or didn't have any contacts, was just check out the classified section of the paper, circle a few that might be interesting and start trying to find them.

I filled out a ton of applications within a couple weeks. In particular, I went to gas stations and movie theaters. I definitely had experience in those places. The problem I ran into with the theaters in both Eugene and Springfield (Springfield is basically attached to Eugene) was that all the projector operators were union jobs. I had learned how to run projectors from my dad and from Neil Dhom. Neil was one of the best operators you were ever going to find. He was so calm and in control at all times, no matter what may have happened. Film had a tendency to break from time to time, the sound would go out, or the light from the carbon arc lamp would flicker or the carbon could break. But Neil was always calm and under control, and he tried to teach me to be the same way.

I didn't have a problem about being a union operator, but there were really no openings to speak of, and if I would have gotten a job, I would have been just a fill in or only work a couple nights a week. I really didn't want to do that. I needed full time employment. So the search went on for a job, and I was getting a little frustrated. Everyone was very supportive of my job search, but I knew I needed to find something soon, and start paying my share for room and board so to speak.

One evening in the paper I noticed an ad that said "Learn Foundation Work." That's about all it said, and gave the guy's name and phone number. I talked to Tom about it when he got home, and my thoughts were that if this guy is willing to teach me how to do foundation work that it might be something that could lead to some good money eventually. Tom and Jane Ann agreed that I should give him a call. Keep in mind I knew nothing about how to put in a house foundation...zero.

So I called the guy and told him that I had seen the ad, and that I was interested in "learning" foundation work. He asked a couple of questions like how old I was, and where did I live—he never asked if I had any experience, or did I have a car. He says "ok well I guess I can give you a try. I'm working in the such and such sub-division in Springfield. Do you know where it is?" I said "no I'm new to the area and my cousin Tom will be bringing me." I wrote down the general area that he gave me, and he says "ok we start at 7:00" and I said "ok I'll see you in the morning." Ok well I had a job. I was going to be learning a trade. That sounded pretty good.

At least for now, Tom was going to take me to work, but I knew that couldn't go on for very long. It wasn't like Tom didn't have anything else to do. The next morning we left about 6:30 am and headed to Springfield in the Buick. Tom didn't want to take me over there in the Bureau car. He really wasn't supposed to have civilian passengers in his Bureau car. We eventually found the guy, and Tom needed to know what time to come back and get me. I introduced myself and ask what time we would be done. He said "well probably 5:00 if we're lucky." I told Tom 5:00 and he said "good luck" and pulled away.

There was really very little conversation. The guy takes me over to where he had poured a foundation. The forms had been knocked loose but were still down in the hole. So he says "alright I need you to pull those forms out and load them on that trailer over there. When you're done with that we need to move them to a different lot and unload 'em over there." And with that, he went to his pick-up truck and drove away.

I began trying to pull the forms up and out of the ground. It didn't take very long for me to realize that I was definitely not in shape for this task. After about three forms my back was already killing me and my legs were getting weak. So I moved to stacking the forms I had removed on to the trailer. By the way, just to be clear, these damn things were heavy and I doubted that they were typically handled by one person. So I loaded the four or five forms on the trailer, and went back to get some more out of the ground. After a couple more, the guy came back to the site. He looks around and says "Christ this is all you got loaded? OK well let's get going."

Just the fact that I was going to have some help was good. I'm not sure how many forms there were, maybe forty, but we pulled them all out and then began to stack them on his trailer. He was less than impressed with my speed and my strength and he made several comments as we stacked those suckers about head high. Finally and thankfully we finished loading the trailer. By that time it was about 11:30 and time for lunch. The guy says “ok we'll take those across the sub-division after lunch.” All I said was “ok” but what I was thinking was “thank God we get a break.”

The guy went to his truck and pulled out his lunch box and a thermos and sat down by a tree. I was just standing there looking rather lost and pitiful at that point, and the guy (I keep calling him the guy because I have long ago forgotten his name) looks up at me and says “Where's your lunch? You brought your lunch didn't you?” and I had to say rather sheepishly “no—I didn't know I was supposed to.”

I know he didn't say what he really wanted to, I could tell from the look on his face, but he said “well I don't leave for lunch. We bring our lunch so....and I don't have enough for both of us so.....I guess you can at least go sit down over there and rest.” Now I'm in a bit of a panic. I hadn't even had a drink of water since I got there and I was really hungry on top of that. I was left with very few choices.

So I mustered up the courage at that point to say “well...uh...can I borrow your truck to go get something to eat?” There was a long pause while he finished chewing a bite of his sandwich. He looks up with a very frustrated look on his face and finally said "well I suppose so, if you weren't smart enough to bring your lunch then I guess that's what I'll have to do." He tells me that there is a little restaurant on the edge of town, about two miles away and there will be a lot of contractors there eating. I said "how long do I have?" and he says "I take a thirty minute lunch so you better get going."

I found my way out of the sub-division to the highway and headed for the restaurant. Sure enough it wasn't far and the parking lot was full of pick-up trucks. The place was small and packed. When I first went in there wasn't even a seat available. I asked a waitress where the restroom was, and among other things, went to wash up. I had dirt and mud caked on my shoes, my clothes, and my hands. I'm not sure I've ever been that dirty before or since. I felt bad about the condition I left the restroom in, but I couldn't help it. I was a mess, and I was in a hurry. I found a seat at the counter, ordered a burger and fries and chugged a couple glasses of water. When the food came I had about ten minutes to eat and get back. I inhaled the food—drank another glass of water—and was on my way.

When I got back the guy was still sitting under the tree, having a smoke. I thanked him for letting me use the truck and he mumbled something as he went to get in the truck to get ready to move the trailer full of forms to a different location. As we're hauling the trailer over across the sub-division, we stopped at a stop sign and another contractor heading the other direction pulled up beside the truck. He says "hey I see you finally got some help." The guy says "yeah but he's not worth much, he doesn't know anything." I'm not sure what was said after that, but probably something about where he was headed with the forms. But that was sure the kind of comment that made you feel even worse than you felt anyway. Man my body hurt in places I didn't even know I had, and then I get openly slammed to another guy while I'm sitting right there. I know I was thinking wow—thanks for the encouragement dude, I really appreciate it.

After the forms were unloaded, cleaned a bit, and laid out around the foundation site, we unhooked the trailer and headed back to the original location. It was actually only about 4:30 when he dropped me off. He said, "So your cousin is coming to pick you up?" I said "yeah he'll be here around 5:00." He says "ok, I'll see you over at the other lot at 7:00 in the morning." I said "ok" and he drove away. I laid down on the ground and waited for Tom to show up. He got there at 5:00 on the nose.

Thankfully my first day of “learning foundation work” was over. I could barely get in the car. I had never hurt in so many places. I knew realistically that my back was never going to be able to do this day after day.

Tom, Jane Ann and I talked about the situation most of the evening. We decided that it would be best if I just called the guy in the morning and told him that it just wasn’t going to work, especially with Tom having to run me back and forth. At 6:00 am I called the guy and told him my decision. He was very nice about it. He said “ok I understand. I’ll send you a check for the day.” I thanked him for giving me a shot, and that was it. My first job in Oregon lasted one day, and I was glad it was over. I took a few more aspirin and went back to bed.

Tom, Jane Ann, Brad, Julie and Brett Ackerman

Part Twelve

Let the Sun Shine In

After a one day stint at "learning foundation work," the job search continued. I was sitting on the couch looking through the "want ads" one evening when Tom got home. He walked into the living room and says Ronj (Ronj was the nickname Tom had assigned to me. He usually had nicknames for everybody.) "Ronj, I think I found a job for you today." I looked up and said "you found me a job—how'd you do that?" He said "well you know that car wash down on Willamette St.?" "Yeah I know where it is." Tom said "well you might want to head down there in the morning. I'm pretty sure they have an opening." I said "how do you know that?" He says "because we picked up a guy down there this afternoon that was AWOL from the Army, so they should need a replacement." I had to laugh at that one. I said "that's cool-- you created a job opening for me—thank you."

The next morning I did indeed ride into town with Tom in the Bureau car. We agreed that it probably wouldn't be a very good idea for him to pull right up to the place in his Bureau car, so he dropped me off about three blocks away, and I walked to the car wash. It was just opening when I walked through the front door to the small lobby area.

A little squirrely guy was standing at the counter. He looks me up and down and says "you need a carwash?" I said "no…I want to talk to the manager." He says "what about?" I said "I'm looking for a job." The squirrely guy says "well I don't think we need anybody, but I guess I can ask him." He went behind the counter and opened a door directly behind it. He just cracked the door and stuck his head in and said something to whoever was in there. After a minute or so he comes back and says "yeah he'll talk to you—his name's Richard." I said "ok thanks" and went around the counter and opened the door.

I stepped in to find Richard sitting behind a very old small desk. The smoke was so thick it was hard to breath, plus the office was just big enough for the desk, Richard and his chair. The large metal ash tray was full of butts and another one was burning in the stack.

Richard was a very large unkempt man, probably about 350 pounds. With no real expression he says "so you're looking for a job?" I said "yeah…I was just wondering if you had any openings." He didn't say anything for several seconds. He just stared and looked me up and down. Finally he says "yeah I might have an opening." "When could you start?" I said "oh...right away...in the morning maybe." He reached in the desk and pulled out an application form and said "here, fill this out at the counter and give it to Billy." Now I knew that the squirrely guy's name was Billy. Richard said "I'll start you at the minimum ($1.60 in 1968 [10]) if you work out I'll go to $1.75." I said "ok that's fine" and turned around to open the door and Richard says "hey—you got a car?" I said "no—but my cousin will bring me into town. He works in town." He said "well...ok we open at 8:00."

I left the car wash and walked straight north on Willamette St. for about four blocks until I found a pay phone. I called the number that Tom had given me. I was actually surprised when Tom answered the phone. I told Tom that I did get the job and had walked to a pay phone. Tom said "well good—where are you?" I told him where I was calling from and he told me he was too busy to come and get me, and that I would have to walk to the post office. The FBI office was in the basement of the main Eugene post office at the time. The post office was quite a bit north on Willamette so I had a pretty long walk but it was worth the trip. Once I got there I got to meet some of the agents that Tom was working with and get a quick look around at the office. I was impressed at the professionalism and courtesy shown to me—a punk kid from a small town in Illinois—with all they had on their minds. I could also sense the great respect the agents and staff all had for Tom even though he was a very young Special Agent in Charge.

Eventually Tom had a little break in the action and was able to take a lunch break. He first ran me back home to Santa Clara and dashed back in to Eugene for some lunch. I even knew at the time that Tom was going way above the norm just to help me out. He certainly didn't have to do that. In reality, he probably wasn't supposed to do that. But out of respect for me, and certainly out of respect for Jane Ann, he did it and I have always been grateful for what he did for me.

On April 29, 1968, HAIR-The American Tribal Love Rock Musical opened on Broadway. It was the story of "the tribe"—politically active long haired hippies living in the "Age of Aquarius." They were protesting the war in Viet Nam and living in the sexual revolution[11]. Some of the songs from that play became extremely popular. "HAIR"—"Let the Sun Shine In" and "Aquarius" were considered, in many cases, anthems for the young students and other likeminded kids at the time. The play was in many ways simply a reflection of what was happening on many of the major college campuses across the country.

The University of Oregon was no exception to those activities. War protests, vandalism at the ROTC center and speeches encouraging violence by groups such as SDS (Students for a Democratic Society) the Black Panthers, Weather Underground (founded by Bill Ayers) and several others, were present on the U of O campus, and the police and the FBI were constantly monitoring their activity[12].

Growing up in a small town in Jasper County Illinois and attending a small community college, I had never experienced anything like what was going on in Eugene. The U of O had approximately 10,000 students in 1968/69, more students than the entire population of Jasper County. It was definitely a culture shock for me. I went from knowing most everyone in town to not knowing anyone, outside of the Ackerman's and now Jack and Joan Douglas. That would change as the days and weeks went on, but the fact was, I really liked my new life. It was so much different and certainly exciting because of the university and what a city has to offer. The thing I missed the most was having friends that I could call and just go have some beers and maybe go listen to a band. The fact that I was still underage and living with an FBI agent and didn't have my own wheels did complicate things a bit, when it came to going out for beers and/or dating.

Tom and Jane Ann were great though, about letting me use the Buick when I needed to. And the fact that I now had a job made it even more important that I find some kind of affordable transportation. But that would have to wait for a while. I needed to save some money first, and I needed to start paying some form of rent to Tom and Jane Ann. They hadn't taken me to raise and I needed to do my part.

The next morning Tom dropped me off three blocks from the carwash and I walked in, just as I had done the previous day. Richard and Billy-the squirrely guy-were already there, and before long two other guys walked in. Richard told Billy to go with me to the back (outside) and when the first customer came in, show me what I would be doing. If my memory is correct, there were only two prices; one for vacuuming and wash, and one for just a wash. I think I remember that it was $2.00

for a wash and $2.50 for a vacuum and wash. Either way it was a good deal.

My job was to vacuum the car, if need be, and hook it up to a large continuous chain like track with a piece of chain with hooks on both ends. One hook would fasten under the car somewhere and the other hook would fasten to the larger chain in the track.

The best description I have for the chain in the track is that it was like a very large motorcycle chain. It was about four inches wide, with links about six inches long. As soon as you hooked the bottom hook on to the track, the car would immediately start moving (provided you put the car in neutral). The car would then be pulled through the wash—different cycles happening as it went. Spinning cloth brushes did the washing and it was rinsed off near the end.

Customers could walk along and watch their car get clean as they looked through the windows. At the other end, when the car had been rinsed off, someone would reach down and unhook the car, another guy would hop in and drive the car forward while a couple of other guys wiped the car off with towels. I found out quickly that the guys in the front were the ones that got the tips, so my goal was to get from the back end to the front end as soon as I could.

I had washed cars by hand for Dick Tracy at Dick's Marathon, so I was aware that Saturdays were the busiest day. It was certainly no different at the automatic car wash. It was crazy on Saturdays. It was pretty much non-stop, and you were lucky to get a bathroom break, and frankly I don't remember what we did about lunch.

What was also different on Saturdays was that Tom could bring me in the Buick and park right across the street. No one could see him from the carwash and they had never seen that car before. It worked the same way when he would pick me up on Saturday evening. No one had any idea who he was, but some people were wondering. Soon the questions would start.

I had worked at the carwash for a few weeks, and since weekdays were not nearly as busy there was more time for conversation. Honestly, I liked it when it was really busy because then I knew that Billy would have other things to do besides talking to me. During cigarette breaks or lunch, Billy was getting very curious about me and why I ended up in Eugene etc. He would usually start by asking me again, where I was from, and how was it I decided to move to Eugene. I had told him several times that my cousin had suggested that I come out and stay with them. Then one day he said "so your cousin brings you in to town every day?" "yeah....that's right" "you can't afford your own car huh" "no not yet" "so where does your cousin work?" I had already thought about this and knew what I was going to say if the question was ever asked. "He works at the post office" "the post office...what's he do there?" "I think he works in the office I'm not sure what he does there though." That was as far as the interrogation went that day. I knew he was fishing for something, I just didn't know what.

A couple days later Billy comes over to sit by me during a break in customers. He leans over and says "hey you know I've been asking you a lot of questions lately" I said "no kidding...what's the deal?" He says "well I just had to know if I could trust you" I said "trust me for what?" He looks around like he was checking to see if anyone was listening and says "do you smoke pot?" I said "why are you asking me that?" He says "I just wondered that's all" I said "well I have before but not much." Billy says "well if you ever want any, I'm your guy." I said "ok...I'll keep that in mind."

So instead of just letting it go at that he says "I got a bunch of it. I have it buried all over my property. I'm a dealer for a lot of people." At this point I started to feel a little uncomfortable. Why was this guy bragging to me about being a drug dealer? I understood now why all the questions about Tom and me and what was I doing in Eugene. I also thought Billy boy, if you only knew what I could do to you at this point, you wouldn't be so confident right now.

He didn't have a clue, and that's the way I needed to keep it. If I had told Tom, and he would have told his friends at the Eugene PD and Billy would have gotten busted—even he and Richard could have put two and two together. And for now, I needed the job.

Part Thirteen

Red Sundown

1968 was the bloodiest year so far in Viet Nam for both American troops and our allies. The Tet offensive was organized by the powers that be in Hanoi in late January, but the official attacks for the offensive were between February 11 thru 17, 1968. Hanoi was determined to strike all major cities and strongholds in the south, including Saigon, with the express purpose of defeating the Allied Forces and totally demoralizing the people in the south. Fortunately for U.S and allied troops, Hanoi's plan was flawed and they payed dearly for it with the U.S and allied troops killing almost 37,000 enemy troops during the Tet offensive. It was also the worst week of the war for American troops with the U.S losing 543 KIA and 2547 wounded[13].

On the home front the news of the Tet offensive shocked the American public as the film and pictures of the offensive were brought into the living rooms across the U.S. As bloody and gory as it was to see, the worst part was that Walter Cronkite, the famed anchor for CBS News, and thought by many to be the most trusted man in America, told his many viewers that the U.S. and its allies had been badly beaten in the Tet offensive and that the U.S. should seek an honorable way to withdraw from the conflict. Naturally many people believed the news reports and it also helped to fuel the anti-war movement and protests on college campuses and in major cities.

And so it was not surprising that the University of Oregon campus was very solidly anti-war, anti-military, anti-government, and anti-Nixon. And, unfortunately, the major organizations and groups behind the demonstrations and protests were becoming more numerous and more violent.

The Black Panther Party membership was growing quickly in 1968. It's presence on the U of O campus was growing quickly as well, and it was not going un-noticed by the FBI or the Eugene Police Department. In fact, the Black Panther Party was not only growing in numbers, it was well known that they were also heavily armed.

The FBI in Washington D.C., at the direction of J. Edgar Hoover, had formed a counter-intelligence operation to start infiltrating the Black Panther Party, and it was indeed a nationwide operation including the U of O campus. There will be more about the demonstrations and protests a little later in this writing.

Because I was now living in a new place, living a very civilian life, my priorities were quite different than my cousin Roger who was still in Viet Nam or my friend Kenny who was now in Ft. Riley KS for surgery and rehab, or for my friend Bruce who was now in Ft. Knox KY for his radio school training, just part of his training before he went to Viet Nam.

Yes, my priorities were much simpler. I was trying to meet more people, not drug dealers, finding out if I could keep a few beers at the house, looking for a better job, and finding a nice girl to hang out with—not necessarily in that order. Also I missed being able to go out for some drinks and maybe listen to some music. The problem was, of course, that I was not twenty one. It wasn't like being able to walk in to Slim's or the Dog House in Dieterich or sometimes the Royal Tavern in Newton, and get a wink and a nod and get served as long as you kept it discreet.

However, I had a plan. Among the clothes that I had asked my parents to ship to me was my suit. I think it must have been my graduation suit. I seem to remember that my mom took me down to Dick Fessel's Clothing in Olney and let me pick it out. I had had them send it just in case I needed to dress up for a job interview. I know that's laughable considering the jobs that I had "interviewed" for at this point. But my plan was to dress in the suit and tie and go into some of the nicer bars downtown, and look different than just your basic college student or underage kid trying to get served. Plus I had on one occasion, while Roger was home on leave from his AIT training at Camp Pendleton, been given a Marine ID.

Roger had at some point had reported his ID missing or lost and the Marine Corps had issued a second one. Yes it had Roger's picture on it, with his hair completely buzzed off, and the picture was not flattering at all, but it was some form of an ID if I got asked for one.

So I had a fake ID from the Marine Corps...and I was living with an FBI agent. Yes, I was a little nervous about that.

As I mentioned earlier, Jack and Joan Douglas lived directly across the street from Tom and Jane Ann. Jack was, to say the least, an interesting guy. He had grown up in Fresno, California where his parents owned a vineyard. When he was seventeen he snuck down to the Marine Corps recruiter and tried to join the Marine's. The recruiter told him he couldn't do it unless he had a letter from his parents giving permission. Jack's parents initially, of course, said absolutely not. After a couple weeks of constant harassment from Jack, even though World War II was raging, his parents finally consented to him joining the Marine Corps.

Jack told me, on more than one occasion, that after he found himself involved in the Marine Corps' island-hopping campaign, hoeing and raking in the vineyard for his dad sounded pretty good. After the war, Jack came back to Fresno and became a fireman. He drove a '67 Mustang 427, four speed. Needless to say he got my attention right away with the Mustang. Jack had his own ways of making his point too.

One of the neighbors next door to Jack had a new dog that had a habit of sitting by the fence at night and barking and howling most of the night. Jack had asked Rich several times to please take care of the situation. After another night of little sleep because of the dog, Jack went to Rich and said "Rich, you either take care of the dog situation or I will." Rich said "what are you going to do?" Jack just said "believe me I'll take care of it."

The next night the dog was at it again. Jack got up, tied two packs of fire crackers together, walked over to the fence where the dog was sitting and barking and lit the fuse. He tossed them over the fence and headed back to the house. As soon as the firecrackers started going off, the dog started yelping and barking and running all over the back yard. By the time the firecrackers stopped popping the dog was silent and cowering under a bush on the other side of the yard. That's where Rich found him. He picked up his pup and took him in the house.

The next day, after Jack got home from work, Rich came over to Jack's house and confronted Jack. He said "Jack I can't believe that you threw firecrackers at my dog. I thought we were friends." Jack said "well we are friends, but I told you that if you didn't take care of it, I would." Rich didn't speak to Jack for several weeks after that, but he also never heard a peep out of the dog after that either. Jack was more than happy to sacrifice speaking to Rich for the good nights of sleep that followed.

Another example of Jack's determination to make his point, again involving a dog, was with his dog Beau. He loved to teach Beau tricks and show people visiting what he had taught Beau.

Apparently, on one occasion, Beau had tired of learning tricks and when Jack called him, Beau apparently guessing that it meant another training session, scurried over and ran under the couch. This happened on a couple more occasions and Jack had had enough of that.

One afternoon the entire family went to Jack and Joan's for a visit. After about a half an hour, Jack couldn't wait any longer, and so he said "hey do want to see Beau's new trick?" Of course we all said "sure." Jack looks around and says "Come here Beau." Beau was not really interested in showing off his new trick, so he made a mad dash to get under the couch instead. Bam...Beau bounced off the bottom of the couch and rolled backwards. He got up and tried it again and bam...he ran into the bottom of the couch again. This time Beau just sat there and looked around like, what the heck is going on.

Now Jack is laughing like crazy, and the rest of us are starting to get what is going on. After Beau's latest session where he ran under the couch and wouldn't come out, Jack drug the couch out to his garage and cut about three inches off the legs of the couch, thus leaving only about an inch between the couch and the floor. So there was no way poor old Beau could ever get under the couch again. Like I said, Jack had his ways.

Fred Bridges was probably one of the first people that Tom met when he came to Eugene. Freddie, as we would all come to know him as, owned the Flagstone Motel at 1601 Franklin Blvd., just off campus. Tom met Freddie while he was watching a suspect who was staying at the motel. Tom and Freddie became good friends, and Tom would later use the motel as a safe house for witnesses and informants that needed to stay out of sight.

Later the Ackerman kids would learn to swim in the pool at the motel[14]. Freddie had a deep and slow Texas drawl and you couldn't help but like him as soon as he started talking. As I would quickly find out, he would also do anything for you if you were his friend.

Freddie was also a musician. He was a keyboard player and he had a small Hammond organ in his living quarters behind the office of the motel. With just a little bit of coaxing Freddie would sit and play the St. Louis blues and old Broadway show tunes and even a gospel tune now and then. The thing that always amazed me about Freddie's playing was that he did it all from memory. I don't ever remember him using sheet music on anything.

Also, I could go down to see Freddie and have a couple beers and not have to worry about anything. In fact, from time to time, Freddie would call a friend of his who was a taxi driver and have him go get some beer and drop it off at the motel. That may have been against the rules, but no one ever had to know about it.

I'll have more about Freddie and the motel later in this writing.

Part Fourteen

Surprise Forecast

One Saturday afternoon in late fall, Tom told me that I needed to get ready and go with him into Eugene. When I asked why, he told me that he needed to talk to Freddie about something, and that Freddie had someone he thought I should meet. So I hurriedly washed up, changed clothes and headed into town with Tom in the big Buick Electra.

When we got to the motel it only took a couple minutes to figure out who Freddie wanted me to meet. When we went in to the lobby, behind the front counter was a rather tall good looking brunette with a friendly smile. Freddie came out of the back—his living quarters—and quickly introduced her to me. Her name was Barb. She smiled and stuck her hand over the counter and we did the obligatory hand shake and said "nice to meet you" and then the rather odd uncomfortable moment when you really don't know what to say next.

I found out later, Tom had already met Barb because Barb's mother (I think her name was

Evelyn) had worked for Freddie for several years. Evelyn was a widow, and very shortly I also got to meet her. It was quickly obvious why Freddie wanted to keep her there for several years. She was so nice and friendly, and would absolutely do whatever it took to keep the motel running smoothly and make sure everything was on the up and up. Freddie did not want anyone to think they could use the motel on an "hourly" basis.

Barb and I became good friends very quickly. It also became evident quickly that Barb was certainly just as nice as her mom was. Barb was actually a few months older than I was, so in my youthful "knucklehead" way of thinking, I thought hey this is cool, Barb will be able to buy beer for us legally in just a few months.

As I began to see Barb on a more regular basis, it became clear that I had to get my own wheels. I knew I needed to do that anyway, but dating with Tom and Jane Ann's car was like using the parent's car. It became pretty uncomfortable to ask for the car, even though I was putting gas in the car and helping to keep it clean, etc. It was also becoming painfully obvious that if I was indeed going to stay in Oregon, I couldn't afford to keep paying on my '63 Chevy SS and just have it sitting in the shed. I was enjoying my new life and the new experiences, but man I missed that car. The thought of selling it was unpleasant to say the least. I had so many good memories about that car, many of which I can't discuss here.

There were ideas tossed about as to what I could do to get the car to Oregon. I could fly home and then drive it back. For me though, financially that was not feasible. My parents could drive it out to Oregon and then fly back. The problem with that idea was that neither one of my parents would fly if there life depended on it.

There were other ideas talked about, such as having another friend drive it out and fly back, but frankly I wasn't comfortable asking anyone to do that. It would have been an approximately 2500 mile drive over a couple different mountain ranges to boot. Realistically there was really only one feasible thing to do. I had to sell the car.

The conversation with my dad about selling the car was downright emotional, at least on my end of the line. I did not want to just put a "for sale" sign in the front window and park it out by the highway at the Fairview Drive-In. I felt that would be totally disrespectful to my car to do it that way. I knew that my friend Kenny was in Ft Riley KS, and I knew that he liked the '63 SS almost as much as I did. I told my dad that before we just put the car up for sale to the public, we had to talk to Kenny first.

I honestly don't remember how I got Kenny's number or what all was said in the conversation, but I do know that Kenny was more than happy to learn that the '63 SS was available. He jumped at the chance to own the car, even though his right arm was fully in a cast and the cast covered most of his upper body. The car was a four speed, and generally shifted with the right hand and arm.

So the details were worked out, and my dad delivered the car to the Yager home. Kenny picked up the car on his next visit home and the car that I had wanted to own from the first time I saw it was headed to a new home.

I was certainly in the market for a different job. The carwash job was not only boring, but the whole situation with Tom dropping me off three blocks away and then either me walking back towards the post office and calling or Tom bringing the family car back in and parking so no one could see him, was just getting to be a little much. Plus I knew that it was a real imposition on Tom as well. And the personnel around the carwash were always a little "iffy." The constant questions about why I was in Eugene and who I was living with had subsided somewhat, but I was ready for a job that was at least a step up from the carwash and hopefully paid more money.

One evening Jane Ann told me that she had heard from a friend that had a friend that knew someone at the Bon Marche Dept. Store that they were looking for someone to help in the display department. I didn't really know anything about the display department, but I knew that the working conditions in a department store like the Bon Marche' had to be better than the carwash.

The Bon Marche' was a large 98,000 sq. foot building at 175 W. Broadway in downtown Eugene.[15] The locals just called it "The Bon." It was a major department store. It carried everything from kids clothing to artwork. The store was known for its fine women's and men's clothing lines, and they even carried clothing for weddings and the fanciest of gowns and tuxedos.

The contact that I was supposed to get in touch with was the personnel director. His name was John Brennan. So I actually put on the suit for a job interview, or at least to fill out the application, and went in to speak with Mr. Brennan. I don't remember every detail, but apparently being able to mention the friend of a friend who knew someone that worked there didn't hurt anything because I ended up getting the job. And as it turned out the guy I would actually work for—the display manager—was also named John, but I don't recall his last name. I'll just call him John A.

It was with pleasure that I was able to go in the next morning and give Richard a one week notice that I was leaving to go to work at the Bon Marche. Of course, he couldn't have cared less. It wasn't like we had bonded and were good buddies. The best part though was getting to tell squirrelly Billy that I was leaving. Now I wouldn't have to put up with any more bragging about his "other" business.

My moving to "the Bon" was also good for Tom. The store was only about two blocks from his office. Tom could literally drop me at the back door of the store, and he was just a couple minutes from his office.

Just walking in the back door of the Bon Marche made me feel that I made a good decision, job wise. It was such a classy place, and the atmosphere was that of "professionalism." People came there to buy apparel to look professional, but the store--with the lighting, the colors, and the displays--made the employees want to be more professional as well. I felt that alright, but I admittedly had a long way to go to be a professional at anything.

The display department was on the third floor of the store. It was sort of tucked away from everything else. When I went to work there, my boss John A and I were the only two people in the display department. There were a total of twenty windows—fourteen in the front and six in the back—to build displays in. Sometimes displays in the front of the store could take up two or three window spaces at a time. Plus there were always the inner store displays for the various departments, so I found out quickly that the display department was actually a pretty big deal. There was really no down time.

Things were constantly changing. My boss was, thankfully, a pretty patient guy. When I started, I knew absolutely nothing about putting in a large window display or how to build an inner store display. John A had to teach me pretty much everything. He was very good at what he did. I had to learn a lot very quickly if I was going to be worth keeping around.

I liked the job for a number of reasons, but one in particular was that unless we were really slammed or some department was complaining that they needed to get a new line of clothing in the window immediately, I didn't have to work on the weekend. That meant I had more time to spend with Barb, plus Tom didn't have to worry about taking me into town on Saturday mornings. And even though I didn't have my own wheels, life was pretty darn good. The thought had already crossed my mind that I might make Oregon my home.

The state of Oregon is an absolutely beautiful state. On clear days you have the view of the Cascade Mountains and to the north a view of the Three Sisters—Mt. Hood, Mt. Rainier, and Mt. St. Helens. The Willamette River flows right through downtown Eugene and the McKenzie River winds around just outside Springfield (just west of Eugene). Parks and recreational areas are everywhere. Needless to say, it offered a lot more than my hometown of Newton, IL.

As far as my lifestyle was concerned, I was actually pretty satisfied. I wasn't drinking very much, although I was getting served in the bars downtown, and I was able to buy beer at the grocery store, sometimes using my fake Marine ID.

I enjoyed spending time with Tom and Jane Ann and Jack and Joan, with Barb and Freddie.

Speaking of Freddie, one afternoon I had gone down to the motel with Barb so that she could tell her mom that we were headed off somewhere (long before cell phones) and we were told by the girl at the front counter that Freddie and Barb's mom were working in one of the rooms, doing some extra cleaning or something.

Sure enough we saw the door open and a cleaning cart sitting outside, so we hustled down to say hi and bye. Barb pecked on the door and said "hello you guys." Freddie comes out and says in his slow Texas drawl "Damn it you two, I've been trying all day to get "Evie" down here to this room so we could have some wild sex, and you guys had to mess it up." Barb and I immediately started laughing and Evelyn was howling as she came out of the room as well.

What made the whole thing so funny was that Freddie would never have done that. He just had a great sense of humor and was always pulling something to make people laugh. Of course Evelyn wouldn't have done that either, she had worked for Freddie for years. The other thing that made it so funny was....Freddie was gay. Everyone who knew Freddie knew that, but if you knew him and knew that he would do anything for you, and that he valued your friendship for just being a friend, you just didn't care. My exposure to gay people had been very limited, plus the fact that I was still very naïve about the whole thing. Living in small town U.S. A. didn't expose you to a lot of different cultures.

Shortly after I started at the Bon Marche, I suspected that my boss John A was also gay. His good friend and "roommate" that came up to visit him a couple times a day was the manager of the lingerie department. Yep... a "guy"managing the lingerie department. Again, a little cultural expansion for me. The final clue for me as far as John A was concerned is, one morning as we were building a display in one of the back windows, I noticed as he was leaned over driving a nail in something on the floor, that showing above the waist of his trousers was a pair of, obviously, women's red silk panties. I'm not sure how long I stood there with my mouth open, but finally I realized that John was asking me for another tool from the tool box, and I had to snap back to reality.

I had already accepted the fact that my friend Freddie was gay, and now I had to just accept that my boss was also gay. And his partner/roommate/co-worker was more than gay. It was quite a bit for a small town, mid-western kid to process in his somewhat culturally limited brain.

Of course when I told Jane Ann about it she said "well sure Ron, don't you know that all the good window dressers are gay?" Actually she said queer, which is what most people were still saying in 1968/69. So I said "well if you knew that why didn't you say something before I went to work there?" She just said "I guess I thought it wouldn't matter." And I guess all things considered...it didn't.

I was enjoying working at "the Bon" and learning something, that before I started, I knew nothing about. I would learn that there was actually an art to building successful window displays. I was learning about how you guided the eyes of the prospective customer to the spot in the display that you wanted them to see. John A was starting to have enough confidence in me that from time to time he would let me build an in store display on my own, and once in a while, a small window display.

I wasn't making a ton of money, but it wasn't bad for the time. I know it was well above minimum wage, and I was starting to save some money. I was also getting very comfortable and more familiar with the Eugene area and what all it had to offer. My main priority was to get a car, and I knew eventually I would have to get a place of my own, or at least share a place. I couldn't stay with the Ackerman's forever.

Part Fifteen

Sun Peeking Through

The next thing Jane Ann surprised me with was absolutely out of left field. I came home one evening and Jane Ann has something circled in the paper lying on the table. Since it was circled in red, I noticed it right away. I said "whatcha got here?" Jane Ann excitedly says "hey you need to check that out. The Very Little Theater is auditioning for a play. You should go down and try out for it." I was caught totally off guard with this one. I said "what are you....I can't do that...I've never done anything like that." Jane Ann said "you did in high school didn't you?" I said "well no...well yeah...but not a whole play, just some stuff with the drama club, and sometimes I didn't even say anything."

Jane Ann says "well you played in a band and you're not afraid of crowds, so you should go down and read for it." She was just not going to give up on it. And now the Ackerman kids, Brad-Brett(Bugs)-and Julie were piling on saying "yeah come on Ron go do it, you can do it." I doubt that they really knew what a play was all about, but they wanted to get in on the fun. So just to get things calmed down a bit, I said "ok-ok when is it?" As it turned out it was a couple different nights the following week. I thought fine, I'll go down to read, they'll find out I have no talent for this and no experience, and they do the standard, ok-well thanks for coming in, and that will be that.

Of course I couldn't just go by myself. Wednesday or Thursday of the following week Jane Ann drove me down to the theater on Hilyard St., just a couple blocks off the campus of the University.

As it turned out the play that was being auditioned was a play by Neil Simon called "The Star Spangled Girl." I found out when I got there that there were only three characters in the whole play, so anyone that got a part was going to be one third of the cast. I sat out in one of the 220 seats of the theater and listened as other people read for the other two parts. The longer I sat there, the more nervous I became. When the director, a lady named Melina Neal, called me to the stage, she told me that I would be reading for the part of Norman. She told me what page to turn to and where we would start.

By this time the script was shaking in my hand. I read my lines and tried to enunciate when I thought it was proper and look at the person reading the other parts. It seemed that the reading went on for an hour, but I'm sure that it was only a few minutes. When I finished, Melina Neal conferred with her assistant Carol Thibeau briefly, and turned back to me and said "Ron can you stay for one more reading?" Although I was surprised, I said that I could. I just assumed that Ms. Neal would say that she appreciated me coming in, and that would be that, and I could go home now.

I read another section of the script with Melina Neal reading the other characters, which lasted for about five minutes. When I had finished, Ms. Neal again conferred with Carol Thibeau. They huddled for a couple minutes, shaking their heads, nodding their heads, talking in a loud whisper, and suddenly Melina Neal turns back to me and says "Ron, we'd like you to play the character of Norman."

I have no question that my mouth dropped open as I stared out in to the seats looking for Jane Ann. I said "sure-ok that's great." I was shocked, surprised, happy and nervous all within about two seconds. I thought, well this is pretty cool actually. No one here knows me from Hoadie's goat, and I got a part in a play. Ms. Neal gave us the dates and locations that we would start reading through the script, starting at her house. She handed out the scripts to me and the other two characters-Andy and Sophie-and it was done.

On the way home Jane Ann says "see I told you that you should do it and look what happened." I said "well yeah...I guess so, but actually I thought I was terrible." Jane Ann of course disagreed, but I expected that. After all it was her idea that I go down there in the first place. So, another new experience begins.

When I called my parents to let them know that I was going to be doing a play, I know they were happy for me, as well as surprised, but I could also sense a little disappointment. I believe that it had to do with the fact that they could tell that I was getting very comfortable in my new world. And then there was the fact that they wouldn't be able to make the trip out to see me do the play, because of their fear of flying.

My parents loved Jane Ann like a daughter, and they thought the world of Tom and of course treated the kids like grandchildren, but I believe there was a slight envy or discomfort with the fact that Jane Ann had asked me to come back to Oregon, and I wasn't even mentioning coming back to Newton or the Fairview Drive-In.

I think my dad knew when I was willing to sell the '63 Super Sport, a car that meant the world to me, that I was in Oregon for more than just a long vacation. I had a great place to stay, I had a girlfriend, I had a decent job, I was making new friends and the scenery in Oregon was beautiful, so what could draw me back to Jasper County? At the time...nothing.

After the Tet offensive in February 1968 and the subsequent reporting from the news media that the U.S. had summarily lost the battle, college campuses across the country had far more war protests and more violence than before. The University of Oregon certainly had some of the most radical groups stationed right there in Eugene. As a reminder there was the SDS (Students for a Democratic Society) their off shoot- the Weather Underground, The Black Panther Party and numerous individuals whose main objective was to incite others to cause havoc in some form.

The FBI and Eugene Police Department were all too familiar with all these groups. When the demonstrations were going on, they were monitoring groups and individuals who may be there to make sure that activities were radical and students were agitated.

From time to time, if the demonstrations were on a weekend, Tom would bring me into town to let me observe some of the protests first hand.

Generally we would do our standard drop me off somewhere, while Tom went to be with the other agents and officers. The FBI was, almost comically, always visible at the protests. They always had on their standard black suits with white shirts and black tie, and their black wing tip shoes. They stood out like a diamond in a...well they stood out. I think they were hoping to be noticed. They wanted the leaders of the various groups to know that they were watching and listening.

One of the “best” demonstrations that I was able to attend had a lot of activity. It started on campus of course, with lots of speakers and cheering and jeering, with lots of protest signs; all anti-war and anti-draft and anti-anything that pertained to the war in Viet Nam or the U.S. government. There were probably close to 2000 people assembled for the event of the day.

The goal of the group was to get the crowd riled and agitated to the boiling point, and then they would march downtown to the city government building, where the draft board was located. There were two major things planned after they arrived at the draft board office. First, a large group of draft age students and general protesters were going to get in a circle outside the building and as a group, burn their draft cards. Also, inside the draft board building was a small group of young men that were scheduled to leave, via bus, and head off to various boot camps. The mere thought of that happening was absolutely unacceptable to the marchers; so they had a plan.

The mass of people marched and chanted their way towards downtown, completely filling the street from side walk to side walk, slowly but surely making their way on the eight block trip to downtown. Of course, traffic was totally blocked, and if some poor soul got caught up in the mess, they were just screwed. All they could do was lock the doors and hope that the crowd kept moving and didn't decide to stop and vandalize the car on their way.

I was trailing along near the very back of the marchers. I was just an observer. I had no dog in the fight, and wanted no part of the protest itself. The cops and some of the FBI agents were also walking along near the rear. Also the Eugene P.D.

was already set up at the destination. It was no secret where they were headed.

So as the throng started to arrive and assemble, the chant of "hell no we won't go" started, and it went on and on, until some of the organizers with bull horns started shouting orders. They were ready to get on with the program. They asked the group of "draft card burners" to get ready for their act. There were probably twelve to fifteen guys that stepped forward out of the crowd, and again with the chants of "hell no we won't go," they in one way or another lit their draft cards on fire and held them up, so that pictures could be taken. And the cheering crowd loved it. Those guys definitely got their fifteen minutes of fame. Even though it was breaking a federal law to burn your draft card, I don't recall any of those guys being arrested that day. You could still be drafted whether you had a draft card or not, this was mainly a way to satisfy the angry protesters, and it worked.

The next act of protest was really the main reason that the mob came down to the induction center. There was a bus parked outside the induction center. The driver was patiently waiting for the approximately fifteen young draftees to come out and get on the bus. Now was the time for the main attraction. Three long-haired protesters came out of the crowd, each with a helper. The three young men sat on the ground in front of the bus; one center, one on the right and one on the left. Their helpers helped wrap chains around their waist and then looped the chains over the bumper of the bus, and fastened them together with pad locks. The three young men were now securely fastened to the bus. Now there's no way the bus is going to be able to take these unfortunate young men to their respective boot camps right.....wrong!

The door to the induction center was opened, and the draftees were escorted out by at least six police officers, and the door to the bus opened and they went quickly on the bus. The protesters were now in a real frenzy. They just knew that they had spoiled the draft board's day.

Within a couple minutes after the young men were on the bus, at least six cops came out of the crowd, three of them with bolt cutters, and promptly cut the chains on all three of the sitting protesters. As the chains dropped to the ground, the cops grabbed the three guys, picked them up and hustled them off to the waiting squad cars. The crowd was now in total shock.

One minute they were ecstatic about the fact that they had achieved their goals for the day, and the next minute the main attraction had gone bust. Now the bus driver was laying on the horn and starting to slowly move through the shocked crowd. The only thing the crowd could do now was boo and boo and boo as the bus went out of sight.

From my stand point the whole thing was both funny and a little scary at the same time. It was scary for the fact hundreds and hundreds of angry people, willing to break the law in order to make their political points, were all around me, and funny because it proved once again that sometimes the best laid plans just don't work out. I guess the organizers had forgotten that bolt cutters existed.

My next move was to walk north on Willamette St. for about eight blocks and meet up with Tom near the post office building. It had been a "good" protest in the sense that, no tear gas had to be used, no weapons were drawn, and the protesters didn't torch the bus. One thing it did remind me of though was the fact that the war was indeed still going strong and my friends and family members were still involved in one form or another.

That particular protest/demonstration was just one of many that were going on across the country on college campuses and in cities, and they weren't going unnoticed by the young men fighting in the jungles of Viet Nam, and those stationed around the world in support operations for the war.

"Stars and Stripes," the American military newspaper, as well as other national publications, was delivered to the troops on a daily basis. The papers were full of the news about violent protests against the war and literally against the people sent to fight it. The troops were very negatively affected by the news that the very people they thought they were fighting for were now violently protesting against them. It hurt. They were fighting a dirty war, in muddy, wet, hot jungles against people, that in many cases they couldn't even see, and now they didn't have the backing of the very people that sent them there.

None of this went unnoticed by the enemy. NVA and Viet Cong troops, captured in battle, carried among their personal papers and orders, propaganda telling them to keep fighting—Americans are losing their will to fight[16]. It hurt.

Bruce Ward-atop armored vehicle - Viet Nam 1969

Part Sixteen

Hotter West Winds

The readings for the play were going very well. Besides Melina Neal's house, we would go to the female leads house, her name was Janet, and sometimes we would go to the other male leads home, his name was Michael, to read and develop the characters' personalities. They were both from Canada, and both had done several plays in Canada as well as Oregon. I was indeed the rookie.

As it turned out, the many meetings for readings to develop characters had another positive development. I had, on many occasions, mentioned that I really needed to find an affordable car, because it was becoming even more uncomfortable to ask Tom and Jane Ann if I could borrow their car. After all I was now dating, had a job, and now was even busier with the play and all that it entailed. One night, while we were at Michael's house, he asked if I was still looking for a car. I told him that I was still looking, and he said "well my wife is trying to sell her MG, maybe it would be something you could afford." I immediately thought of the little MG two seat convertibles that I had seen, especially since I arrived in Oregon. There were several of them driving around Eugene, especially in the campus area. They were pretty cool cars, small, but cool.

So I said "yeah I'm interested in looking at it. How much does she want for it?" Michael thought it was somewhere in the neighborhood of $900.00. We set a time within the next couple of days for me to take a look at it, and went back to work.

A couple days later I drove back over to Michael's house to look at the little convertible. I guess I just hadn't asked enough questions about the car, because when we went to the back of the house to see it, it wasn't a convertible at all. It was a light blue 1964 MG 1100—Sports Sedan. The 1100 stood for 1100 cc's. I opened the hood to find a cross mounted 4 cylinder engine. At first glance it looked as though someone had surely taken part of the engine away. After I stood there and looked at it for a couple minutes I couldn't help but laugh. I was used to opening the hood of my car, the '63 Chevy, and seeing a V8 with chrome valve covers, chrome air breather cover, and a big Carter AFB carburetor staring back at me. Plus, this little two door sedan was front wheel drive.

I absolutely couldn't see myself driving the little car. I'd be the laughing stock of the neighborhood. Jack had the 427 Mustang and Tom had the big boat of a Buick with a huge V8, probably at least 400 cubic inches—not cc's—inches. The MG did have a 4 speed transmission, but the little shifter was pitiful compared to the Hurst shifter I was used to. The '63 SS, after Alan Dale and I changed the cam, was probably putting out about 325 to 330 horsepower, and I find out that this little MG 1100 puts out all of 55 horsepower. Man if my buddies back in Jasper County found out I was driving something like that, I could never live it down. Plus it didn't even have a radio. I thought, how do cars not have a radio, that's just ridiculous.

So I said "hey Mike I appreciate you showing it to me, but I just don't think I can do it—plus I wouldn't want to give $900.00 for it." "And it doesn't have a radio—I really need a radio in the car." Michael says "yeah I get that, but it gets unbelievable mileage, probably 40 miles per gallon and it's got a sun roof, so it's almost like a convertible—plus you've got a back seat." "Let me go see what she'll take for it." I said "ok, go ahead and ask her." So now it's almost like being at the dealership and the salesman has to go in and see what the boss will take for it. And usually the salesman comes back out and says "well I really had to work on him, he didn't want to do it but yeah he'll take "whatever" for it."

Sure enough Michael comes back out and says "well she really wanted $900.00 for it, but since it's you and it doesn't have a radio, she'll take $800.00 for it.

I thought, wow what a surprise, because it's me she'll take $800.00 for it. I thought about it for a second and decided to do it. I desperately needed wheels of my own. It should be pretty cheap transportation, at 40 miles per gallon. I could surely install a radio, and hey, it did have a sunroof and a back seat. And it would just be my little secret, as far as Roger and Kenny and Mike and my other buddies were concerned. They just didn't have to know what I was driving.

The on stage rehearsals for "The Star Spangled Girl" started in early January. We had about two weeks before opening night was upon us. At home, I was using Jane Ann to play the other two characters and give me my ques. Memorizing all the lines was more difficult than I expected, but between Melina Neal, the other cast members and Jane Ann helping me, everything was beginning to click.

The amount of work involved to put on a play, even in a small community theater is hard to believe. Besides the cast and director and her assistant, there were the set designers, and then the set builders. The set director and the prop manager all had their specific jobs. Also as our dress rehearsal night approached, I had to do something that I had never done before. I had to learn how to put on make-up. That's just not something that I had ever had to do or wanted to do so far in my life. Michael was very helpful in teaching me what to do. He had done several plays and was an old hand at putting on the stage make-up. It wasn't really that hard.

For the information about the cast members that went in the play bill, I was asked how many plays I had done and where I was from. Well the amount of plays was actually zero, but they didn't want to put that information in there, so we put down that I had done some plays in high school. As far as where I was from, I said "Newton, IL." and the lady said "where's Newton, IL.?" and I tried to give her an idea what part of the state it was in, and she says "well what big city is it near?" I said "well it's not really close to any big city" and she says "well what's it closest to?" I said "I guess it would be St. Louis." So sure enough, when the play bill was printed, I was from the "St. Louis area." I guess Newton, IL was just not going to cut it.

Our opening night, if memory serves me correctly, was to be Wednesday January 15, 1969. So our dress rehearsal was on Tuesday night. Only a few members of the media, a couple photographers, and members of the crew were allowed in the theater. Even though it was only a dress rehearsal, the local theater critic was in the audience. He was also there for opening night, so I guess he must have critiqued us on both performances. Anyway, the dress rehearsal was successful. Everyone knew their lines, and if you happen to forget a line or didn't pick up on a que, someone off stage would prompt you. It was actually a pretty professional operation.

Opening night jitters are a common occurrence even amongst the big Broadway stars, so it was no surprise that we all were experiencing a little nervousness as we got dressed and ready backstage. I suspected that the experienced cast members and Melina Neal might have some additional edginess just wondering if the rookie—me, would lock up once the curtain went up. I actually never felt that way. I think the fact that I had played in a band and performed in front of crowds helped me to not be overly nervous. I tried to remember that no one is actually sitting out there hoping that you screw up—they actually want you to do well, for the most part. And most in the crowd are glad they're sitting out there watching, instead of being on stage in front of a crowd anyway, so that all helped.

Opening night went very well. We had lots of laughs and a lot of applause from the audience. The people who came back stage afterwards were very complementary and encouraging. Melina Neal was thrilled and told us all that we had done a great job. In fact, Melina popped a bottle of champagne after the meet and greet was over, and we all toasted ourselves for a job well done.

But that was only one night. We were scheduled to do a total of ten shows, so there was a lot of work ahead. We did shows on January 15- 16-17 and 18 that week. I thought that actually every show was better than the last. We were then scheduled to do shows on January 22-23-24-and 25. The final two shows were scheduled for the next Friday and Saturday. Everything was going really well, possibly better than expected, and it seemed that we would cruise through all the shows with no real problems. That was true until the weekend of Jan. 25 and 26.

Part Seventeen

Quite White

The weather forecast for the weekend of January 25-26, 1969 was for a couple inches of snow. It started snowing early in the morning on Saturday, and by the time it stopped late on Sunday evening, the total was somewhere between 43 and 46 inches. It snowed 23 inches in the first 24 hours, and just kept going[17]. The flakes were huge and wet and they clung to everything they touched like soft fluffy magnets. Within the first couple of hours the streets were all covered and pretty much impassable.

Almost to a person, in our neighborhood at least, people were either standing by their front windows, or standing on the front porch and just watching it snow. It was the heaviest and most intense snow that anyone had ever witnessed. Growing up in the Midwest, I had seen some pretty significant snow storms, but I too had never seen anything like this before. The snow was so heavy that you could barely see Jack and Joan's house across the street.

The Ackerman kids were naturally amazed and excited about what they were seeing. They wanted to do what most kids would want to do when they see that much wet snow coming down at that rate, they wanted to go out and play in it. In fact, I too thought it would be fun to go out and at least throw some snowballs for a while. Sure enough Jack came outside and we were chucking snowballs back and forth across the street at each other. And there was certainly no one out scooping the sidewalks or driveways. At the rate the snow was falling the driveway would be totally covered again by the time you finished trying to clear it off.

The snow was mesmerizing to watch. I think most people were sure it would be stopping soon, because, after all, the forecast was for about two inches for the weekend. But it went on and on. By Sunday afternoon the snow was around three feet deep, and still showing no signs of stopping.

As beautiful and record setting as it was, the reality of what was coming after the snow finally ended, was beginning to set in. Eugene and Springfield, and in fact all of Lane County, was going to be paralyzed for the most part. I seem to remember that Lane County had all of three snow plows for the entire county, which geographically was very large. It stretched all the way to the coast on the west and to the east it went all the way to the Cascade Mountains and covered the Willamette National Forest. The snowfall amounts were absolutely unprecedented and the county and state officials were all caught off guard.

The Willamette valley, however, was the recipient of the largest amount. The questions started to pop into peoples' mind as Monday morning finally saw the end of the record snowfall. The questions were about the basics. How are we going to get our groceries? How am I going to get to work? How will the police and ambulances get around? The answers were all about the same—nobody knew what was going to happen. The Willamette valley had never experienced anything like this....ever.

The Ackerman family and I were fortunate to have enough food for a few days, but the basics like eggs, bread, milk, and at the time, cigarettes were going fast. There was no way we were going to get the car out. Even if we would have dug a lane out of the drive way, the streets in the sub-division had four feet of snow on them. Across the street at the Douglas household, the situation was about the same. They weren't going to starve to death, but the thought of both of them running out of smokes was more than they could bear to think about. And as crazy as that might sound now, this was 1969 when most everyone smoked. Not that the groceries weren't important, they certainly were.

On Tuesday Jack called the house and said that he had heard that a snowplow had been down River Road. It had opened up one lane, but the trucks that supplied the small grocery store on the corner of River Road and Irving Road were able to get through. The problem for us was, that was probably at least a half a mile away, which if you were driving was just a couple minutes—no problem. But we weren't driving. The plan was to take turns digging a path out to Irving Road. If we were lucky possibly the snowplow had been on Irving Road as well, we had no idea.

So Jack, Tom, and I started out with back packs on and short grocery lists from our respective homes as well as a couple of the neighbors. We took turns digging and shoveling our way out to Irving Road, hoping and praying that either a snowplow or a county truck or something big had broken a track on that road so we didn't have to dig all the way down to the grocery store.

When we finally got to Irving Road we were all elated to find that "something" had indeed been through and had broken at least a track that we could walk in. We had certainly had enough digging and shoveling for that day. In fact, I was hoping I never had to do that again in my life.

As we expected, the little grocery store was packed with people, and the stock was pretty sparse. We grabbed what we could from all the various lists—jammed it in our backpacks and headed back to our neighborhood. The walk back was smooth compared to the "walk" out.

We delivered and divided up the groceries for us and the neighbors. If we were only able to get one dozen eggs for example, but three people had ordered a dozen, then we would share that dozen amongst everyone. We bought quarts of milk instead of gallons. Not only because of the weight, but at least everyone had "some" milk etc. And those who smoked may have gotten brands that they were not familiar with, but at least they had some smokes. Again, I know it sounds crazy now, but that's just the way it was in 1969.

I had already experienced things in Oregon that I had never imagined, and now I got to experience a historic record snowfall that not even the native people of the Willamette valley had ever seen, or had to deal with. It would be talked about, and stories told about it for generations.

I believe that it was at least Friday before a snowplow finally came down and opened the street in our neighborhood. Fortunately the temperature was getting warmer, and some melting was taking place, but what a mess. The streets and roads were slushy and rutted for days. When the cold would set back in at night the slush would re-freeze. It made it pretty much impossible for my little MG 1100 to navigate even though it was front wheel drive. But I finally got it out of there and made it back to work on the following Monday February 3rd. Everything had been shut down so it wasn't as though we had missed a lot of customers or needed to worry about changing out the windows.

It had been an unbelievable week, and all the conversations that went on for several days after that were all about the snow, and what people did to cope, and how neighbors were helping each other out and sharing what they had etc. It was really something—something I'll never forget.

Needless to say the shows at the Very Little Theater had been cancelled during the shutdown. We had been scheduled to do three more shows when the snow hit. We did those shows on

Thursday-Friday-Saturday, February 6-7-8 if my memory is correct. As we finished the last performance and went back stage to celebrate, director Melina Neal approached us and said that members of the board of the theater had asked her if we would consider doing three more performances. She said the board felt that the show was doing well enough that it could support the additional shows, since we had sold out almost every performance.

We all agreed that absolutely we would do three more shows. Personally that was something I hadn't even thought about. I knew we were filling the place up, but I never expected to get an "encore." After all this was my first legitimate play. The following Wednesday-Thursday-Friday we did our final three "held over" performances. Amazingly they were all sold out as well. We had done a total of thirteen performances, which was unusual for that theater. The cast and crew all worked very well together, and I have always been grateful to Melina, Carol, Michael and Janet for their professional guidance.

If it hadn't been for Jane Ann's encouragement and prodding I would have never even gone down for the reading. I was certainly glad that I had done that. I also realized that I enjoyed the interaction between the other players and the audience each time I was on stage. I knew that it was something that I wanted to do again. I hoped that the people casting other plays for the Very Little Theater would consider me in the future. I had another experience that I probably never would have experienced in Jasper County. Maybe I had actually found a direction.

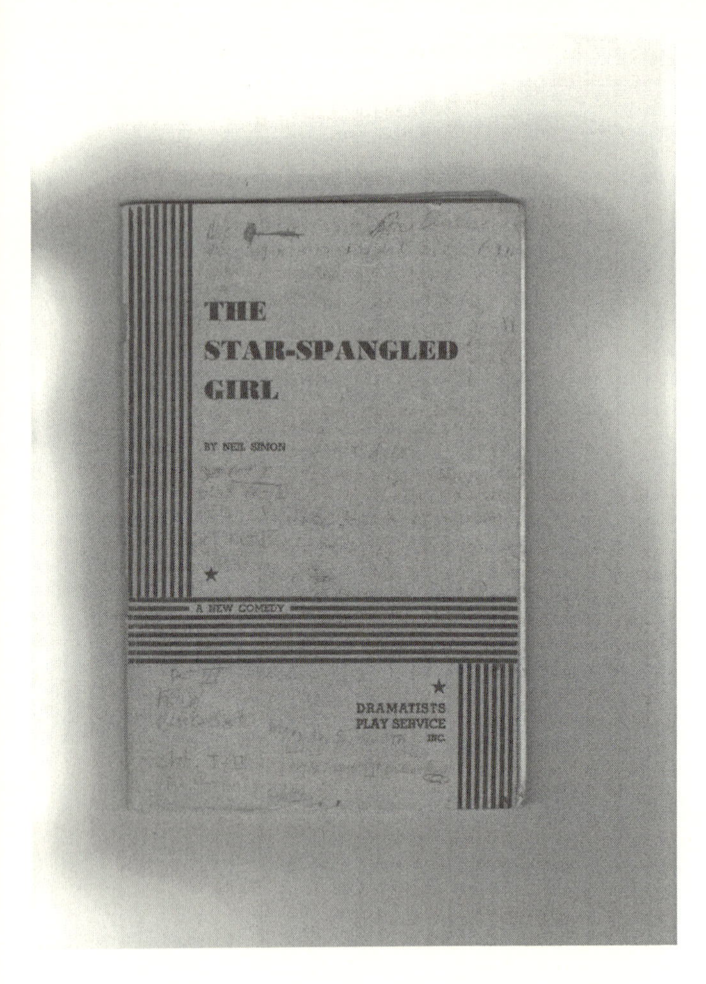

Original script from the play "The Star Spangled Girl" in 1969.

Part Eighteen

Sunshine before the Fall

The first priority for me and the little MG 1100 was to get a radio. There was a plate on the dash that appeared to be where the radio was "supposed" to be, so I knew approximately what size it was supposed to be. I got in touch with a guy in downtown Eugene that worked on foreign cars and had him order a radio for me. He knew which radio was standard for the car. As soon as the radio came in, I asked Jack if we could use his garage to install it. Jack had all the tools we would need for the job.

I bought an antenna for the radio at an auto parts store, and as far as I knew I had everything I needed, and it should be about a two hour job. Tom, Jack and I started the job of installation after supper. It looked like it should be a relatively simple job. But as I had already observed earlier in life—NOTHING is ever simple.

When we got the cover plate off, we found a solid piece of plastic/polyvinyl running the entire length of the dash. I honestly don't remember how long it took us to cut out the approximately 3 inch by 6 inch chunk of the plastic/polyvinyl, but it was a struggle. Then there was the wiring. How do we make sure that we got to the proper circuit, without having a schematic of the car? What could possibly go wrong? It seemed like hours before we found the proper wiring harness and got the radio to at least turn on.

The antenna should be no problem right? All we needed to do was attach the thing to the back of the radio, run the cable through the dash at some point near the passenger side fender, cut a hole in the fender, run the cable up there, screw the thing on and viola—turn the radio on and enjoy the tunes right. Wrong. I suppose that it all had to do with quality, noise control and all that, but there was no way that cable was going through all the dirty, rotten, stinking, go*#$m, good for nothing sheets of plastic/polyvinyl to get to the passenger side fender.

By this time it was approaching midnight. We were all tired, frustrated, angry and amazed at how much of the plastic compound the British Motor Corporation, makers of the MG 1100, had put in the vehicle. None of us had ever seen anything like it. Since the antenna cable did fit in the proper hole, I said ok guys, "just leave it the way it is. I've got a radio and I'll just stick the antenna out the sun roof when I'm driving." Jack and Tom may have been tired, but they both busted out laughing. Jack said "are you serious, you're going to just hold on to it and stick it out the top?" It was late and I knew we needed to end this project on a good note, so I said "yeah I'm serious, why not?" So the job that should have taken two hours took five, but at least I had a radio and we were able to end on a funny note.

One morning about a week after we had installed the radio, I was driving to work with my sunroof slightly open, holding the antenna with my right hand, and listening to some "Deep Purple" if I remember correctly. I caught a glimpse of a green Mustang coming up behind me. I knew at that time in the morning, it more than likely would be Jack and Joan heading in to work. The Mustang came creeping up beside me, I looked over to see Jack and Joan both smiling from ear to ear and nodding in acknowledgement that yes, it was funny, but it worked.

Admittedly it was a little unhandy when I had to shift, but if I was in town and going slow enough, I could sometimes close the sunroof on it and it would stay put while I was shifting. And Barb was, fortunately, a really good sport about it. She never gave me a bad time when I would ask her to hold the antenna while we were driving. No—I'm pretty sure she was thinking—"my hero" he's driving a 55hp, four cylinder, front wheel drive power house car—AND—he lets me hold his antenna out the sunroof for him. I mean really, what more could she ask for?

The little MG was cheap transportation alright, but it had a tendency to "nickel and dime" me a lot. Besides the radio, I had to replace the generator, and the dimmer switch, which was located on the floor board, as most cars were at that time. I found out my dimmer switch was bad while driving home from the play one night. I had my bright lights on and someone was flashing at me to dim my lights. As soon as I hit the dimmer switch, the headlights went out completely. I was a little shocked to say the least, and I'm sure the guy who flashed me was too. I hit the dimmer switch again and fortunately the lights came back on. I thought, wow, this is an interesting situation. I can't wait to tell Jack and Tom about this one. And I knew Barb would be very proud of what the little car could do now.

Barb's twenty-first birthday is something we had both been looking forward to for several months. I had decided that I wanted to take her to a nice restaurant, for a nice meal, and of course a couple of cocktails in celebration of her twenty-first. The restaurant was in a hotel between Eugene and Springfield. We were both dressed well for the occasion. Barb looked very nice.

A nice young lady seated us and after the pleasantries, asked us if we would like something to drink. I smiled at Barb and said "you go first" and Barb ordered a cocktail, and then the young lady looks at me and says "and you sir" and I ordered a cocktail. All of us are all smiles at this point. And then the waitress looks at Barb and says "may I see your ID please?" Now Barb and I are really smiling, and as Barb reached in her purse for her ID. I said "that's what we're here for. This is her twenty-first birthday celebration." The waitress was now not smiling. She looked at Barb's ID and said, "Oh I see—this is actually your birthday today." Barb said "yep...finally made it." Then the waitress says "well I'm really sorry, but since this is just your birthday today, I can't serve you."

Now I had to say something. I said "wait a minute; you're saying that because it's her birthday you can't serve her? Now that she's twenty-one you can't serve her?" "That's the most ridiculous thing I've ever heard." The waitress is now looking at Barb and trying to explain what the deal is. "Well it's just our rule, that if it's just your birthday today, we can't serve you alcohol." Barb was such a nice girl and never looked for a confrontation of any kind. She really wasn't up for an argument. I on the other hand was definitely ready for an argument.

I was the one sitting there with a fake ID, which by the way the waitress had not even asked me for my ID. I said "look we chose this restaurant for a nice evening to celebrate her twenty-first birthday and you're going to spoil the whole thing with a ridiculous rule like that. I want to talk to your manager." The waitress says "well I can see if he's available." I said "good, you go see." Barb says "look, its ok-- we'll just go somewhere else." I said "oh we're going to go somewhere else alright, but not 'til I tell the manager how stupid this whole thing is."

Finally the waitress comes back and says "he's not available right now, but he says that the reason we do that is, we don't know exactly what hour you were born, so it may be that you're not really twenty-one yet." I was absolutely speechless...for about ten seconds. I said "it's now about 7:30 in the evening. So you're telling me that maybe Barb wasn't born until 10:00 or 11:00 o'clock at night, and you're afraid she might not be quite twenty-one, and you can't serve her a cocktail on her birthday." She says "I'm sorry but that's just our rule." So I said "fine, you tell your manager that we think it's the stupidest damn rule we ever heard of, and we'll go spend our money somewhere else."

To this day I've never heard of a rule being enforced anywhere like that. Barb and I were both sort of out of the mood for a fancy meal, so we found a Safeway store and went in and bought some beer and some snacks. When the lady at the checkout asked for an ID, I let Barb show hers. The lady looked at Barb's ID and says "oh it's your birthday...well Happy Birthday hon." Barb just said "thank you." I was tempted to go in to the restaurant story, but I didn't say anything.

Neither of us could think of anyplace we really wanted to go, so we decided to just go to "my house." We couldn't wait to tell Jane Ann and Tom about our evening out. I knew Jane Ann would have a lot to say about the situation.

On the way there, driving on I-5 headed for Beltline Road, a truck flashed me to dim my lights. I instinctively just hit the dimmer switch. I didn't have a chance to warn Barb about my latest problem. The headlights went off immediately, and Barb says "holy mackerel what's going on?" I said “yeah—I hadn’t had a chance to tell you about this little problem yet.” She said “well turn ‘em back on for crying out loud.” I messed with her for about a half mile, acting like they wouldn’t come back on. But it was fun. It was always fun to mess with Barb—she was so innocent and sweet. So we went to “my house” and had our beer and snacks. It was a nice celebration after all.

Part Nineteen

A Little Less Spring

Early in the spring of 1969, a Eugene high school football star had been killed in a car crash near the Oregon-California border. If that wasn't tragic enough, it was discovered that he had a large amount of drugs in the trunk. The entire Eugene area was shocked and in disbelief that the young man was in any way involved in running drugs. He was smart, talented, had a bright future, and had a good family relationship, so it was hard for the community to accept that he had gotten involved with some of the scum bags in the area. I guess the money must have been the big magnet that drew him in.

My job at the Bon Marche' was actually going pretty well. John A. had a little more confidence in my ability now, so on occasion he would let me help design and plan a display. But...not lost on me or my friend Bill, the part time employee and future Marine, was the fact that John A. was gay. The reason for bringing that up again has to do with a situation that Bill found himself in, and needed John A.'s help in getting out of.

On one of the occasions that someone needed to work late on a Friday, Bill had drawn the short straw. He had gone to a small restaurant for his supper break that was located about a block from the store. If you went out the back of the store it was an easy five minute walk. Bill sat by himself at the counter, and ordered a simple meal-something he could afford-probably all of a couple dollars. When he went to the cash register to pay, an adult male probably forty years old, steps up and says “hey, why don’t you let me get that for you?”

Bill looks up and says “what, you want to buy my supper?” The guy, who was dressed in a nice suit says “sure let me get it” and has the cashier add it to his tab. Bill didn’t really know what was going on, but he did know that he just saved a couple bucks on a meal, so he was good with it. He thanked the man, and walked outside and headed back to the store. Bill had only gotten about fifty yards when the man in the suit shouted at him. Bill turned around and stopped and the guy asked where Bill was headed. Bill told him he was going back to work at the Bon Marche’. The guy says “do you mind if I walk down there with you?” Bill told him no- he didn’t mind, so the man walked to the back of the store with Bill. Bill went to the employee entrance, and opened the door, thanked the man again for buying his meal and started to walk in.

The man in the suit says "do you mind if I come in with you, I need to use the restroom?" At this point Bill is becoming a little suspicious and a little defensive. Bill told him that the restrooms were around the corner behind the stairs. At that point the man in the suit says "would you like to come in there with me?" Bill says "come in there with you…hell no I don't want to come in there with you. What do you think I am some kind of queer or something?" "No I have to go to work and you better get the hell out of here right now." And with that Bill sprints up the stairs to the third floor, looking behind him at each level. The man in the suit did not follow him upstairs.

When Bill told me that story on Monday, he also added the dramatics of what he would have done to the man in the suit had he followed him upstairs. He had a large cardboard box, and demonstrated how he would have punched him, while swearing loudly at the box as he knocked it down two flights of stairs. It was hysterical. He was so proud of himself as he carried the box back upstairs.

The problem was that wasn't the end of it. Later that day a phone call was transferred to the display department for Bill. He had apparently told the man in the suit his name, and he called him at work. Bill was really angry when he found out who was on the phone. He quickly told the guy to never call again, and hung up. We both knew that we had to tell John A. about the situation.

During the afternoon while John A. was sitting in the office, we both went in. Bill started telling the story, and before he was even finished John A. asked about the description of the man. Bill described him and John A. said that he knew who it was. John A. said "I'll take care of this, and don't either one of you do anything stupid in the meantime."

We assured him that we wouldn't do anything more about it, but we were both curious as to who the man in the suit was. John A. explained that he had known him for a long time. The guy was the display manager for a large furniture store, just a couple blocks from the Bon Marche'. He was married and had two children. John A., surprisingly, told us that the man knew when he got married that he was gay, but to maintain an image, he got married and had children. Again, it was a lot to absorb for a kid from Jasper County IL.

But John A. was right, he took care of it, and Bill never heard from the man in the suit again.

A little later that spring John A. had given me the responsibility for building an inside department display. He told me the colors that he wanted, but other than that it was my baby. The colors of paint that I would need had to be blended by the paint store, so one afternoon John A. sent me to the paint store, which was about five blocks from the "Bon." As I walked along Broadway heading for Willamette Street, I looked up to see a semi-familiar face headed right for me. Before I could make any form of evasive move, he was right in front of me. It was squirrely Billy from the car wash.

Unfortunately he had recognized me as well. He says "hey you're the guy who used to work with me at the car wash right?" Reluctantly I said "yeah that's right." He said "yeah you're working down at the Bon Marche ain't ya?" I quickly said "yeah that's right and my boss sent me to the paint store to pick up some paint, so I better get going, see you later." Billy said "oh yeah sure...hey you heard about that kid that got killed right—the football player—down by the state line?" I nodded that yes I had heard about it, and hoped that was the end of the conversation.

Squirrely Billy got a look on his face that was somewhere between indignation, disappointment and bragging. Without looking me in the eye, he says "yeah that was a shame about that kid. He was one of our best "mules." "He was really a hard worker." Even though I was still a naïve twenty year old from the Midwest, I knew what he was talking about, and I knew that this low life standing in front of me was only sorry that he and his group of drug dealers had lost a good worker.

Billy had no concern for the family or the friends of the kid who was killed, only for the fact that he was a good "mule." I can't even describe my feelings at that point. Anger was certainly part of it, but I had to take into account that this guy wasn't above making the whole story up. With no expression I simply said "yeah...it is a shame. I gotta go." Billy said "ok man see ya." Thankfully that was the last time I ever saw squirrely Billy.

I continued my walk to the paint store, all the while trying to get the story and Billy's face out of my mind, but it was not easy.

I gave the color swatches to the guy at the counter of the paint store, and mentioned that my boss had called about getting these colors mixed. Within a few minutes he brought the two gallons of paint to the counter. It was a charge for the Bon Marche', and I was on my way back. I had given no thought at all about how much a gallon of oil based paint weighed. As it turns out it was over eleven pounds each[18]. It wasn't bad for the first block, but by the second block I was beginning to feel like a real wimp.

At the end of the second block I had to set the cans down and rest my arms. By the end of the third block, I was wondering why in the world I hadn't gone to get my car for this trip. By the time I got into the fifth block, I was hoping that there weren't people watching me, because I was only making it about a hundred feet at a time before I had to set the darn cans down again. I thought that if my old football coach, Frank Chisevsky had known about this, he probably would have substituted it in place of duck walking. It would have gone something like "alright Kinder that was the worst block I've ever seen in my life. Go get those gallon paint cans over there and start walking around the track until I tell you to stop." By the time you made one trip around the track, you would have been begging him to just let you duck walk.

When I finally made it back to the store, I could barely lift the cans up on to the work table. John A.

came out of the office and said "everything go ok, what took you so long?" My arms were dangling down at my side like a couple pieces of rope, and I certainly didn't want to mention the encounter with squirrely Billy, so I just said "well it took the guy at the paint store quite a while to mix the paint." I don't know if he bought the story or not, but he just said "well ok, let's get started on that display downstairs." I thought, well I won't be much help with no arms, but ok. Man I was glad there was only a couple hours left in the day.

My arms hadn't felt that bad since my day of "learning foundation work".

It's difficult to explain the difference in my lifestyle while I was living in Eugene. Even though I knew very few people, there was calmness in my life that I hadn't really felt before. The pressure to be out drinking and partying at every opportunity was gone. Tom and Jane Ann had been very patient with me when I didn't have a job or even have my own car. Barb and I had a pretty good relationship going, although I was, admittedly, trying to get her to spend more time with me, rather than with her other friends. I guess that quality of wanting to be too controlling had not gone away. I actually liked my job, even though I knew it probably wouldn't be a career position. All in all, things were going well, and I had no real intention of going back to Illinois other than to visit my parents and friends from time to time.

Melina Neal and Carol Thibeau, director and co-director, of the play had given me a heads up about the new community college that had opened in 1965, but in 1967 had expanded in size physically and in the number of students.[19] The primary reason for mentioning Lane Community College to me was that they were supposed to have an excellent drama and theater department, and Melina knew and highly recommended the department head. It certainly piqued my interest. I had given some thought to starting classes there anyway, and if I could get involved in a good theater class, and do a better job of concentrating on making better grades, it would be a good change for me.

Within a couple weeks I made the trip down to 30th Ave. and found the registration office at Lane Community College. I frankly don't remember all the classes that I registered for, but definitely the drama classes were number one on my list. Of course, I had to have my records from Olney Community College transferred out there, such as they were. I had a lot of work to do just to get enough credits to qualify as a sophomore.

But believe it or not, I was ready to do it. I even surprised myself in the fact that I was actually looking forward to going back to school. Just a few months earlier it was the last thing I ever thought would happen. I had been in a place that was pretty dark and out of control. I didn't miss that place. I really didn't want to go back there again.

So it was set. I would work through the summer, save some money, and start classes in September. I was also aware that as cool as it was to live with the Ackerman family, I couldn't stay there forever. Once I got settled in school, I needed to find someone to share a place with. It was just another reality and it had to be done.

I had not been very good about writing or calling my parents. I didn't have a very good excuse for not doing that, other than that I was busy with quite a few things, but so were my parents. That excuse didn't really hold water, I knew that. Part of my failure to communicate on a regular basis had to do with the fact that I was having a good time and was finally feeling comfortable in my skin.

I did talk to Roger and Kenny from time to time. By the spring of 1969 they were both back in the states, but were still in the Marines and Army for the time being. Bruce Ward however was just leaving for Viet Nam on March 16, 1969, so the war was still on my mind.

The U of O campus was still a busy place as far as the protests and demonstrations against the war, and pretty much anything that was associated with the Nixon administration. The U of O campus had become a solid home for the SDS, which had become a violently revolutionary group. The SDS, along with the headquarters of the Black Panther Party in Eugene, was always on the radar for the FBI as well.

Tom Ackerman, as the agent in charge for the FBI, dealt with these groups on a daily basis. And although he couldn't just come home and open up about who and what was happening, a few tidbits of information would sometimes be discussed. The Black Panthers knew that the FBI, on a national basis, was trying to infiltrate the group with informants to keep the FBI and local police abreast of any violent or disruptive activities. It was well known that the Panthers were armed, and willing to use it.

The image of the FBI agent in his suit and wing tip shoes was not necessarily the total story. There certainly were days and weeks at a time when Tom, and certainly the other agents, were working day and night, not even coming home to sleep. It was not glamorous. It was simply hard, tedious, and many times dangerous work. It was the "other side" of the war that the public usually never heard of.

So even knowing the small amount that I did, as far as Tom's responsibilities, I was always grateful and thankful that Tom did so much to help me, especially when I didn't have a job or a car. It would have been understandable if he would have said "sorry Ronj you're on your own." But he never did. He was always willing to help.

Jane Ann had three young children to take care of. She was constantly cleaning, cooking, doing laundry, running the kids to school or the doctor. Our family relationship was strong, but she would have had every right to say "hey Ron, maybe you should think about going back to Jasper County." If she ever thought it she never said it. In fact, Jane Ann was always encouraging me to try new things and she was always there to talk to me about whatever my current crisis may be. And sometimes she would be brutally honest, but that was Jane Ann. If you didn't want to hear her answer, then don't ask the question. But I wouldn't have wanted it any other way.

The Ackerman kids also had a serious change to deal with when I moved in. All of a sudden a twenty year old "big brother" had shown up. It had to be quite an adjustment for them as well. As I had mentioned earlier Tom loved to assign nicknames to everyone, thus my nickname of "Ronj." The kids had also been assigned nicknames—Brad was "Burfurd" or just "Burf." Brett was always "Bugs" or "Bugger." That name had stuck since Brett was a very small child. Someone sat a Christmas present up in front of him and his eyes bugged out—thus "Bugs." Julie was either "Jules" or "Puff." Most of the time we all called her "Jules."

And even Jack Douglas didn't escape the nicknaming. Tom assigned him "two smoke." I believe that was in reference to the dual exhaust on Jack's Mustang.

Part Twenty

A Change in the Forecast

In early April my dad called the house, and after a short conversation with Jane Ann, and asking about the kids and Tom etc., my dad asked to speak with me. I got on the phone, and after our standard questions of how everyone was doing and the weather etc. my dad paused for a while. I thought possibly we had lost our connection, so I said "Dad, are you there?" He said "yeah...yeah I'm here...uh listen Ron, I need you to come home and help me run the drive-in for the summer."

Now I was the one pausing. His statement caught me so off guard that I didn't know what to say. I knew my dad wouldn't ask me to do that if he didn't really mean it. When he said "needs me to" it was straight forward and not hard to understand. When I started talking again I said "well...uh...yeah I guess I will." "You know I have a job out here...and a car...and a girlfriend and all, right?" He said "yes I know you do, but your mom and I talked about it, and we really need you to come home and help run this place."

The drive-in theater business is not an easy business, I knew that. During the summer and early fall, it is a seven day a week business. No holidays and its rain or shine. I knew all that, and frankly it was one of the reasons I decided to check out Oregon and a different lifestyle. The difference in my lifestyle had certainly been a drastic, but needed change.

I told my dad that I would give notice at work, and let them know that I would be back in the fall. I also told him about being registered for school again. He and my mom were both happy to hear that I was interested in school again, but happier to know that I was coming back for the summer. Quite frankly I was less enthusiastic about it.

I had a long and rather painful conversation with Jane Ann and Tom about the situation. Jane Ann was almost like a daughter to my parents, so she understood their point of view and, as always, she was supportive and honest with me about it.

The whole thing was a shock to me. Just as I thought I was really getting my stuff together, it was going to have to be put on pause. I was certainly not looking forward to trying to explain the situation to John A. and John Brennan at the Bon Marche'. I could only hope that they would somehow work with me to consider it a leave of absence. I had considered the fact that I had a steady job an important factor when I considered going back to school.

And I really was not looking forward to telling Barb that I was going to be gone, back to Illinois, for probably four months. However Barb was very understanding about the whole thing. She lived with her mother and older brother, and was a good Christian girl. She understood that family has to come first. I felt lucky to have met her and spend time with her.

When I got to sit down with John A. and John Brennan I was pleasantly surprised that they both felt the same as Barb did about family coming first. They couldn't promise me that I would be able to come back to the same job, but John Brennan said that they would do their best to find a position for me when I got back. That was a relief.

Sometime around the second week in May I packed some clothes and not much else, and headed back to Illinois for the summer. My parents paid for the airline ticket. I had said my good-byes to Tom and Jane Ann, the kids, Jack and Joan, Freddie, and of course Barb and her mom. I told everyone that I'd see them in the fall when it was time to get back for classes at Lane Community College.

I told Tom to drive the MG once in a while, and use it whenever he needed it. Tom drove me to the airport, which was only ten minutes away, and I was gone.

The Eastern Air Lines Boeing 727 "Whisper Jet" sat down on the runway at St. Louis Lambert Field on time in its flight from Portland. I never really knew why Boeing called the 727 a "Whisper Jet", it seemed to be as loud as any other jet, but I guess it was a smart marketing tool. I don't remember what day it was when I got back, but that afternoon my dad was able to come down and pick me up.

As was the case every time I walked in to the terminal after coming off the plane, my dad was there smiling and he would give me his customary greeting of "Hi—boy was I glad to see that thing get on the ground." Nothing had changed about his opinion of airplanes. He couldn't understand how they got off the ground, and he had no intention of ever getting on one.

The conversation between us lasted most of the way home. My dad wanted to know what I had been doing, and what the Ackerman's were up to, and what about the kids etc. Eventually of course the conversation had to turn to the Fairview Drive-In. During the spring-summer and early fall, the work at the Drive-In was pretty much non-stop. There was always something to work on. It may be maintenance on the mowers, the tractor, the ice machine, the deep fryer, the projectors, or just generally cleaning, but it was always there.

The fun part of the Drive-In business was of course the movies. 1969 offered some great movies, and many were available for running at the Fairview. "True Grit" with John Wayne, Glen Campbell, and Kim Darby. "The Wild Bunch" with William Holden, Robert Ryan and Ernest Borgnine. "Support Your Local Sheriff" with James Garner and Walter Brennen. "Easy Rider" with Peter Fonda, Dennis Hopper and Jack Nicholson. "Alice's Restaurant" with Arlo Guthrie. And later that year "Paint Your Wagon." Actually what turned out to be the Academy Award winner for Best Picture was "Midnight Cowboy" with Jon Voight and Dustin Hoffman; to this day one of my all-time favorite movies. The reason that some operators wouldn't run the movie is because the Motion Picture Association of America had given the movie an X rating, which was generally associated with pornography. Those operators, my dad included, just didn't want the "negative publicity" in their theaters. I later saw the movie with my friend Greg Crouse in a theater in Olney. The X rating was way overblown in my opinion.

When we arrived at the Drive-In, and pulled through the grounds toward the house, I couldn't help but feel a little nagging, slightly haunting feeling of the dark days that had led to my leaving Jasper County in the first place. I didn't want to dwell on it and I didn't want to relive it, but something was there anyway.

Of course my mom was glad to see me. It had been several months. She had basically the same questions about Oregon, Tom and Jane Ann and the kids as my dad had asked, but it was ok, we went through it all again. My dad wanted to show me all the changes that he and my mom had made in the concession stand, and get me reacquainted with the projectors and how to put a show together etc. I hadn't really forgotten how to do it, but I would be rusty for the first few shows.

On May 2nd 1969 Kenny Yager was officially discharged from the U.S. Army. He had undergone more surgery and rehabilitation at Ft. Riley, and was completely free of any cast on his right arm. I don't remember just how long it was before we got together for some beers and stories, but not long.

It was rather surreal to be the passenger in the '63 Super Sport that up until a few months ago, I was driving. It also didn't take long to get back together with friends Alan Beard, Mike Yager, Art Hunzinger and the other Nite Raiders members. Greg Crouse and Jeff Dalton were still around, but on March 6, 1969 Elmer Zumbahlen, former bass guitar and sometimes rhythm guitar player, left for a two year stint in the Army. Fortunately he did not end up in Viet Nam. He spent most of the time in Korea, at the DMZ.

As good as it was to see everyone and get back together and have beers and swap stories, an old pattern started to develop rather quickly. I also was falling back into the rather complicated situation of dating three different girls. As soon as I got back to town I had contacted "Ruby" to see if there was a chance at reconciliation. Also within a short time I had rekindled a relationship with "Brandi" and had also given a call to "Alice." When I contacted "Alice," to see if she wanted to go out again, she was not interested. So I said "well wait a minute "Alice" I have grown up a lot since I've been gone." "Alice" said "yeah I've grown up a lot since you've been gone too, that's why I don't want to go out with you anymore." I wasn't really expecting that, and it created even more of a challenge. I couldn't let my ego be damaged, so I didn't give up. I kept calling and asking and promising to do better this time. Eventually and reluctantly "Alice" decided that she could give it another try.

"Ruby" was the only one of the three that I had actually maintained any serious contact with while I was in Eugene. We had exchanged some letters while I was there, and admittedly she was the one I hoped to spend the most time with while I was home, even though it would only be for a few months.

Meanwhile at the Fairview Drive-In the season was getting into full swing. My responsibilities for the season were to keep the grounds and concession stand clean, keep up with the mowing, both the push mowing and on the tractor with the bush hog. I ran the projectors three to four nights a week and would work at the box-office whenever I was needed. Neil Dhom was the other projector operator, and both Neil and I had responsibilities of putting shows together. Putting shows together meant going through each twenty minute reel to make sure that the film wasn't broken or the sprocket holes hadn't been torn up by the last projector that had run the film. You also had to make sure that the last operator had actually rewound the reel, so that when you put the reel on the projector, it wasn't running the thing backwards.

If the film was broken or damaged, you had to sometimes cut out part of the reel and re-splice it, and then hope that the film didn't break during the show. Inevitably though, there were films that broke. At that point, it got rather chaotic in the projection room. Once the film breaks, you have to get the projector stopped as quickly as possible, so the projector doesn't continue to "eat" the film. After the broken film was cleaned out of the projector, and rethreaded, and put on a new pick up reel, you were almost ready to start the show again. But the old carbon-arc projectors weren't as simple as just turning on a light bulb.

The carbon bars had to be re-struck and adjusted to make sure the light was going to be bright enough. Then turn on the projector and turn the damper handle down and hope for the best. Of course in the meantime, while the chaos was going on inside—outside the patrons were expressing their dis-satisfaction that the picture was off the screen by honking their horns and flashing their headlights. It was as though they thought that someone in the projection booth was playing a nasty trick on them, like “hey watch what happens when I turn the projector off for a few minutes.”

It was every operator’s nightmare that it happened three or four times in one night. And sometimes because of recklessness or pure laziness by some operators, who didn’t care what condition the film was in when it left their theater, it would happen over and over again. Some of the old prints that had been around for years were very susceptible to breakage.

My dad’s work ethic and pride in his work would not allow that to happen at the Fairview Drive-In. He wanted the film that left there to be in at least as good a shape if not better than when it got there. If the film was “rotten” and torn up, he would have us put a note in one of the film cans to warn the next operator about it. I’d like to think that at least some of that work ethic and pride in a job well done, rubbed off on me.

As the Drive-In season got busier, the number of parties and opportunities to get together with old friends, both male and female, got busier as well. There were also four members of the once very busy Nite Raiders band back in the area. Kenny Yager, Greg Crouse, Jeff Dalton and me. I suppose it was inevitable that we would, at some point all get together and play some music again. Soon we were rehearsing and playing some of the old material, and learning new songs, just like we did before the break-up.

Kenny was excited about getting to play again, and we all understood why. I'm sure there was a point that he had to wonder if he would ever play the guitar again. It seemed that all of us had matured, at least musically, and we were able to get into a little more substantial and difficult music than we were before. It was great to be back with the old group. And soon Yager's basement was the "headquarters" for the Nite Raiders band once again. Having Kenny back and playing again was a double gift. Our friendship would become even stronger than before.

Part Twenty One

Slightly Overcast

One of the problems about being home for the Drive-In season, with plans to return to Eugene in the fall, was that I was again without my own wheels. I could use my parent's car for dates, which at the time was a 1968 Oldsmobile Delta 88. Surprisingly, my dad had bought the car that had the Rocket 455 engine in it. Even with just a two barrel carburetor on it, it was rated at 310 hp. He probably never told my mom how big the engine was. All she knew was that it had one, and it got her back and forth from the Drive-In to Newton.

The Olds was big and heavy, and never meant to have a great deal of speed from a dead stop, but man when that thing got shifted through the four speed automatic transmission, and hit the top end, it was a smooth ride with a lot of speed to offer. It was actually fun to drive. The "Drive-In" or the work/hunting car was a 1959 Ford station wagon, six-cylinder, three speed on the column. It hauled hunting dogs, film canisters, lumber, and now drums and other band equipment.

My friends were very good about hauling me around though. And as if I didn't have enough things going on that summer, one day I asked my friend Alan if he would mind taking me to Sullivan, IL to find the office of the Little Theater on the Square. I had given it some thought, and decided that if I could do a play while I was home, it would give me just that much more experience for when I got back to Eugene and started classes. So one afternoon, Alan and Artie and I headed for Sullivan, so that I could let those folks know that I was available for casting in a play.

We found the office after asking a young man where it was. It was on the north east corner of the square. It was anything but fancy. The three of us walked in and were greeted by a young man and a young lady. The young lady asked if she could help us, and I said "yes…I'm from Newton and I'm home for the summer, and I was hoping that I might be able to do a play while I was here." The young man said "oh…ok do you have any experience?" I said "yes earlier this year I played Norman in "The Star Spangled Girl" in a theater in Eugene, Oregon." He said "ok… have you done anything else?" I said "actually…no, other than some dramatics club stuff in high school."

At that point the young lady said "well can you sing?" I said "no not really." She said "can you dance?" I had to say "no." She said "well, all of our shows this season are musicals and really, we already have our summer stock people signed on for this year, so I don't think we would be able to use you this season...sorry."

They were both very nice about it, and it was obvious that I was definitely not qualified. We all said our good byes and the three of us left. It was a blast of cold air on my hot idea about doing something there. I did quickly realize that I had a lot to learn about theater, and when I started the drama classes at Lane Community College, I may be the least experienced person in the room. So, it was back to Newton to concentrate on the things that I did have a lot of experience in. Working at the Drive-In, drinking beer, playing music, and dating girls. That was a road that I knew very well, and it always seemed to go in a big circle and come back to the same place. And then it started all over again.

The Nite Raiders were back in the saddle, and itching to get back to a regular schedule of playing for people. We may not have been back to the level of perfection or as "tight" as we were before the break-up, but we were getting there. By mid-

June we had started booking some jobs, and it felt good to be back out playing and getting re-acquainted with some of the people and places that we had played before, as well as finding new places. It was going to be a busy summer.

As the band started booking jobs and getting back in the groove of playing, we heard about a "battle of the bands" that was going to take place at the Coles County Fair, I believe sometime in July. We knew it would be a struggle to get ready for that competition, but after hearing the lineup of the bands, we thought we might as well give it a try.

The band that worried us most was The Curiosity Shoppe from Effingham. That is one of the bands that played in the "battle" that we had to cancel, when Greg unexpectedly went to Texas. Most of us had heard this band play, and man they were talented. Their vocals were outstanding and musically, they didn't have a weak spot. But, the Nite Raiders had faced tough competition before and we had prevailed, so we were looking forward to the challenge.

I remember that evening, for whatever reason, we were caught off guard as to when we were supposed to play. We had not even carried our equipment across the race track from the parking lot, and as we were watching The Curiosity Shoppe play, someone came down to where we were standing and asked "are you guys the Nite Raiders?" We in unison said "yeah, that's us." He said "well you guys are next, so be ready to set up when these guys are finished." Holy Crap. I think we all panicked at the same time, and took off across the race track to start carrying equipment back across the track.

It was hot and dusty, and now we're sprinting to our cars to get equipment. I guess we thought we were playing much later, but that didn't matter now. And why we were all parked across the track instead of in the infield, I have no idea. And bands didn't play for an hour during "battles" usually it was just a few songs, so we were in a predicament for sure. It was even less than organized chaos as we tried to get set up. By now all of us were sweating profusely and running into each other as we tried desperately to get ready to go, and not totally interrupt the program. After all, the crowd was waiting to hear more music, and the judges must have been thinking—Is this their first time playing or what?

Finally we were ready to play. Not really ready, but we had no choice. I would have given $10.00 for an ice cold beer at that moment. We checked our set list and got started. Admittedly, we were a little frazzled. By the third or fourth song we finally got settled down, but by that time we had been through most of the set. We finished pretty strong, but The Curiosity Shoppe had been flawless. I think we all knew that we were in trouble.

When the "battle" was over, the MC made the announcement of the runner-up and the winner. We weren't the runner-up, and the winner, to no one's surprise, was The Curiosity Shoppe. Points-wise we had finished third. It was disappointing and a jolt for us. We had finished first in every "battle" that we had competed in, but it was a reality check for all of us. It made us very aware that we needed to get to work, and get back to the quality band that we had always been. Again, reality is a cruel mistress, but sometimes she makes her point very obvious.

On March 16, 1969 my friend and classmate Bruce Ward had shipped out for Viet Nam. So even though I wanted to forget that the war was still going and that the U.S. still had 475,000 troops on the ground[20]it was always there in the back of your mind. Roger left Viet Nam on December 11, 1968, so he was already back in the states and had been assigned to the Marine Corps Finance Center in Kansas City by the time I got home from Oregon.

When Roger got home from Viet Nam in mid-December, he had something waiting on him that was both beautiful and a little dangerous. It was a 1969 Plymouth GTX, 440 Magnum with a four-speed. It was Forest Green with a black vinyl top and white leather interior. It was the epitome of a muscle car. It was rated at 375 hp out of the factory, but who knows what the real number was. Manufacturers at that time were trying to keep the power ratings down, so the insurance rates wouldn't prevent their target market buyers from being able to afford to own one. It didn't always work.

Roger, like a lot of men that had been lucky enough to return home from war, was a little more out of control than even we were before he left for the Marine Corps. Frankly, neither one of us had any business in a car that could go that fast. I seem to remember that it would run 140 miles an hour flat out. I'm not trying to be an analyst, but looking back on those days, it seems as though many of us were living very, very close to the edge. In some cases, teetering very close to the tipping point.

On June 18, 1969 PFC Harry D. “Buddy” Gowin was fatally wounded by enemy mortar fire near Cam Lo, Quang Tri province, Viet Nam.[21] I was originally told that “Buddy” died as a result of a land mine, but that was incorrect. “Buddy” was the first person that I knew personally, to die in the war. “Buddy” was a childhood friend and playmate when times were a lot less complicated for “kids.” Roger and I had some great and fun times with “Buddy” in Falmouth, where his grandparents lived.

Many times “Buddy” would join in on some experimental projects that Roger and I had devised, only to find out that it may have been more dangerous than fun. If he was hurt or “banged up” due to the fact that he just wanted to be a part of whatever we were doing, he never let it stop him. He may have had to sit out for a little while, and rub his head or his leg, or whatever got injured, but within a few minutes he would be right back at it, hanging out with the “big” kids. “Buddy” was one tough little kid, and it was no surprise to me that he joined the U.S. Marine Corps. I have no doubt that he was a tough Marine as well.

On June 25, 1969 Corporal Roger L. Kinder was given his orders to report to the Marine Barracks, U.S. Naval Base in Philadelphia. From there he received additional orders to continue to the U.S.

Air Force Base at Dover, Delaware, report to the Mortuary Officer as the escort for the remains of PFC Harry D. Gowin. Corporal Kinder was responsible for the safe return of PFC Gowin's remains to the Flagg Funeral Home in Newton.

The fact that Roger was escorting "Buddy" back home from Dover was in itself surreal. That's not the way it was supposed to be. It was great that Roger was able to do so, but we were used to picking "Buddy" up after he fell out of a tree or after he fell off a horse, not this. Reality is a cruel mistress.

After "Buddy's" full military funeral and burial in the Bailey Cemetery in Wheeler, Roger's temporary duty as escort was over. He was to return immediately to the Marine Corps Finance Center in Kansas City. There was no time for popping a few cold ones and remembering the good and simple times that we loved to talk about. And how tough a little kid "Buddy" was, and how much fun we used to have. Some of us were able to do that, but it wasn't the same.

The Crystal Club, between Teutopolis and Effingham, was one of the hottest bar and music scenes in downstate Illinois. Gene and Joanie Hartke were the owner/operators of the club. It was also one of the most desirable places for bands to play. If you were good enough to get the job there, it meant that you would be playing both Friday and Saturday night. The patrons at the Crystal Club had come to expect the bands that played there to be really good, and have a great set list. The Nite Raiders were fortunate enough to land a regular slot there.

We played every fourth weekend, and on some of the holiday week-ends. And as long as you kept bringing the patrons back, and they stayed and danced and most importantly for Gene and Joanie, drank, you kept your spot.

Newton bands were well represented at the Crystal. Our old friends- The Illusions- also had a regular slot. They earned it. As always their show was tight and professional.

It's been too many years ago for me to remember the other two bands that had regular spots at the Crystal, but I know they had to be able to bring in a crowd, or Gene would find someone else. Gene and Joanie were good business people. They knew how to get people in the door. The bands' job was to make sure they stayed. It was just that simple.

The summer of 1969 was a combination of very good news and very bad news, both nationally and locally. And the music of the era was changing drastically as well. Janis Joplin had started her solo career, and was absolutely going places musically that our generation couldn't believe. Led Zeppelin, Jimi Hendrix, The Rolling Stones, Buffalo Springfield, Three Dog Night, were all producing music that young people couldn't get enough of. Local and regional bands were trying to keep up with the demand, but some of the sounds that were coming out of the stereo speakers or your car radio were seemingly impossible to re-produce, but bands had to try to do at least some of the material to keep the crowd satisfied.

The "evolution" of music that was going on seemed to be following the "revolution" that was happening on many of the college campuses around the nation. The amalgamation of groups protesting the war in Viet Nam, the Nixon administration, poverty, treatment of African-Americans, treatment of Native Americans, and the U.S. government in general was growing and getting louder and more violent on a daily basis. Newspapers, magazines, and the national TV news reports were never lacking for stories and photos and film of the latest chaos happening across the U.S.

Those stories and films also made their way to North Viet Nam and to the Viet Cong. As mentioned earlier, the enemy used that to encourage their troops to keep fighting, because the U.S. had lost its will to fight, and the Americans were weak. Not only was it demoralizing and discouraging to our troops, but the parents and families of those on the ground in Southeast Asia now had a new problem to worry about.

Many returning soldiers were being harassed and spit upon when they got off the plane and walked through the airport with their uniforms on. As news of this ridiculous phenomenon reached the troops still in theater, many soldiers upon reaching the U.S., would dash into the nearest restroom and change out of their uniform into civilian clothes. In most cases this would protect them from being spit upon, called “baby killers” or “murderers”.

Never before, in the entire history of the United States military, had returning troops had to endure such disrespect from their fellow citizens. Being angry at the U.S. government and military policies is one thing, but to berate and dehumanize the very people who were fighting for their country, and doing what they had been trained to do, was something that I could not believe was happening in the United States of America. And frankly, to this day I still can't believe it.

So, as if the parents and family members of their returning sons, daughters, brothers, cousins didn't have enough to worry about, now they had to be concerned about how the returning family members would react to their treatment "after" they got home. Many reacted by simply keeping themselves numb. Some came through it all with little or no bad effects. But many took their hurt and bad experiences to their grave, and never got it all out.

The transition from living a relatively simple and innocent life was, for some, swift and brutal. In most cases the young man who stepped off the bus at their basic training center, was never going to come home with the same thoughts about life or death, as they had when they stepped on to that bus.

Recently I spoke to Marie Ward, Bruce's mom, and she told me that her friends had told her that they felt that she and Don (Bruce's dad) had aged ten years, the year that Bruce was in Viet Nam. I'm sure that she speaks for hundreds of thousands of parents that felt the same way. That transition affected parents as well.

Part Twenty Two

Wet and Wild

On Sunday evening July 20, 1969 as Kenny Yager and I drove back to Newton from Dieterich in "his" '63 Super Sport-- I'm sure we had been on a beer run-- we saw the crescent moon coming up in the southwestern sky.[22] We were both so proud to be talking about the fact that the United States had put men on the moon. Later that evening both of those men would actually set foot on the moon.

We made our way to the Fairview Drive-In, and into our living room, in hopes of watching Neil Armstrong come down the ladder and actually step on to the moon's surface. My dad had taken a break from his duties to come over and watch as well. At about 10:00 central time[23], we got our wish. Neil Armstrong came slowly down the ladder of the lunar module, and with a little jump to the surface became the first man to ever set foot on the moon. It was for most Americans an "Oh my God-I can't believe it" moment. I know that I just sat there speechless for a few minutes, beaming with pride for all those that helped in completing the mission that President John F. Kennedy had wanted to see happen before the end of the decade, and we—the United States of America—had done it.

I couldn't help but believe that even those who thought they hated the U. S. government had to be proud that evening. Yes, the war in Viet Nam was still raging, but for those few days and specifically those few minutes, there was no war, and there were no violent demonstrations, or U.S. cities on fire, there was only pride and a sense of accomplishment for the United States of America. If only we didn't have to come back to reality here on the planet Earth, how nice that would have been, but reality is a cruel mistress.

As the summer of 1969 moved along, I was doing my best to keep up with my tasks at the Fairview Drive-In, the increasing amount of gigs for the Nite Raiders, the ever growing party scene, and ongoing situation of dating three different girls. I was frustrated and disappointed that I was not able to spend more time with "Ruby," but I was beginning to realize the unfortunate reality was that, she didn't want to be with me nearly as bad as I wanted to be with her.

I suppose that I was using my disappointment as the best excuse to drink even more beer or spirits. And then an especially nasty situation compounded the problem. My friend "Sam" went through a divorce. Once that was finalized, the lid came off of rational, and soon became ridiculous—for both of us. Bitterness and anger abounded and we were bound to drown it, one way or the other.

Many long nights of washing away whatever it was that we were trying to wash away came about. I never missed a night's work or a Nite Raiders gig, or my responsibilities during the day at the Drive-In, but I also probably dealt with a hangover on a daily basis. "Sam" and I saw the sun come up on several occasions, and it wasn't because we were going dove hunting. There were certainly times when we were out of control and out of bounds.

To give you an idea of some of the stunts that we pulled during that period—there was a nice lady, who happened to own a package liquor store, and she lived in the back. She would allow some of us to drink in the living quarters as long as we behaved ourselves and didn't cause a commotion when customers were up front. One night after "Sam" and I had been there for several hours, we decided to go out back and see how the horse was doing. We petted the horse, we talked to the horse, and at one point we even tried to get on the horse, but that was not happening—thankfully. So if we couldn't ride the horse, then the next logical thing to do—said the two drunks—was to see if we could get the horse in the house to hang out with us in there.

Now I don't know if you've ever tried to get a horse to go through a regular size door made for human beings, but it's not easy. In fact we found out that it is pretty much impossible. Even though we encouraged it to lower its head and duck under the top of the door, the horse was just as determined not to do that. After several minutes of laughing and trying to assist the horse through the door, and a lot of clomping and whinnying from the horse, the nice lady came to the back door, and upon seeing what the two drunks were trying to do—unleashed holy hell on the two drunks.

She had every reason to do that. She told us in very explicit terms to take the horse back to the pen, get whatever we had left in the house, and hit the road without delay. I cleaned that up considerably. But, she did let us come back on other occasions, and that is certainly the last time we tried to bring the horse into drink with us.

On another occasion during the drink-fest that "Sam" and I were on, we ended up at the Crystal Club after several other stops along the way. We were sitting on the lower level, by the dance floor. I had apparently lost track of just how many rum and Cokes I had consumed, and upon finishing another one, I sat the glass down on the table, looked over in the corner, and told "Sam" that I was going to throw a "hand grenade" over in the corner. He looked down at the glass—figured out what I meant—and said "no Kinder don't do that, you'll get us kicked out of here, do not do that."

It was too late, my mind was made up. I just knew it was going to be hilarious. I chucked the glass over head in a high arch right into the corner—CRASH—glass flew everywhere. I was already laughing my drunken butt off when I noticed that "Sam's" glass was empty too, so I grabbed it and while "Sam" was hollering "don't do it you dumbass, we're gonna get kicked out of here" I heaved it over my head in a perfect arch in to the corner—CRASH—again glass went flying all over the floor. As I again laughed my drunken butt off, I noticed all the tables around us were now staring at me, and "Sam" was not laughing at all. As I turned my head to the right, I noticed someone was leaning on the table and looking directly down on me. I looked up to see Gene Hartke staring at my face, and certainly not smiling.

He said “Kinder do you enjoy coming here to drink?” I finally got out a very serious “yes.” He said “Do you enjoy playing music here with the band?” “Yes” “Well let me tell you, if I ever see you do something that stupid in here again, you won’t be drinking or playing in here—do you understand me!?” I said “yes I understand you.” He said “ok then, behave yourself” and he turned and walked away. “Sam” was half smiling and shaking his head and said “you dumbass, I told you not to do that.” I knew it was time to go home, so we made our way out. I tried a drunken apology to Gene on the way out.

The next day I realized that I had crossed the line—big time—I knew that I could have really screwed things up for the band, myself, and several other people. I truly believe that, that particular incident was the peak of my drunken stupidity, although there was one other occasion that too many rum and Cokes caused me a serious problem one night at “Alice’s” house.

I had taken her home and was sipping on a beer when I needed to use the rest room. As I finished in the restroom, I started to feel really dizzy. I got the door open, and was making a mad dash back to the couch when I completely blacked out, going through "Alice's" bedroom, and hit the floor like a sack of cement. BAM—I crashed on the floor. I woke up immediately, only to hear "Alice's" dad holler "ALICE" is everything ok?" "Alice says "yeah he's ok, he just tripped coming through the bedroom." I thought oh man I've got to get out of here before her dad comes out with a ball bat, or worse.

I went outside immediately and sat on the step for a little while. I took a few deep breaths, apologized to "Alice" and hit the road. Those two incidents did truly make me realize that I had to slow down. I was teetering on the edge again. I thought that during my time in Oregon I had lost that person, but he was back. It was definitely time to lose him again, and soon.

Part Twenty Three

Better Weather Ahead

3 Days of Peace and Music...Woodstock. August 15 thru 18, 1969. The biggest and most historic music festival to ever be assembled, was held at Max Yasgur's 600 acre dairy farm—White Lake, near Bethel, New York[24]. Woodstock was actually 43 miles away. But it didn't matter "where" it was held; it was "what happened" there that made it the greatest music festival of all time. No one, certainly not the organizers and promoters, could have imagined the outcome.

The traffic just trying to get to the actual location in southwest New York was a nightmare. The cars, vans, pick-up trucks and buses were so backed up that eventually people just started abandoning their vehicles and started walking, not knowing for sure how far it was to the venue. Eventually, the crowd of hippies, attorneys, mothers, fathers, store clerks, you name it, amassed into a crowd of somewhere between 450,000 and 500,000. By the time the first acts went on stage on August 15, the gate and fences had long since been overrun.

The mass of humanity that gathered there was unbelievable, and so were the 32 different groups and artists that performed at "Woodstock." The acts included Arlo Guthrie, Santana, the Grateful Dead, Janis Joplin, the Who, The Band, Joe Cocker, Crosby-Stills and Nash, and Jimi Hendrix. Most of the artists were brought in by helicopter, because the roads were all so jammed up with abandoned vehicles. On top of that, Mother Nature was not cooperative. A long downpour made the large fields a muddy, slippery mess. That did not dampen the spirits of the partyers however. They continued to dance and scream, share their drugs with their neighbors, and enjoy the tremendous event that they were a part of.

"Woodstock" was another defining event for the 60's generation. Believe it or not, there was no violence, no looting or political demonstrations. Aside from some nudity and general "bohemian" behavior, it was indeed "3 days of peace and music." There were only two deaths reported. One from a mishandled insulin injection and the other when a tractor ran over someone sleeping in a nearby hay field.[25] From that time forward, outdoor music festivals would never be the same. The entirety of that festival had an impact on all musicians and I dare say all types of bands. I know from my perspective, it made me want to get on stage and play for more people, in more places. As a musician, you just couldn't help but get excited about what you had just seen.

As August began to wind down and the new school year was approaching, I had a decision to make. I had to either let my parents know that I was indeed heading back to Oregon to start the new school year there, which would also mean leaving the band, or I had to defer leaving for this semester, and look forward to starting school in the spring semester.

After much thought and looking at all the possibilities and angles, I made the decision to stay in Jasper County through the winter. That also meant I had to call Tom and Jane Ann and let them know what I was doing. As far as I knew, they were expecting me back by the first of September. My car was still there, parked in front of their house and I had told Jack and Joan, and my boss at the Bon Marche, and Barb that I would see them in the fall. I wasn't looking forward to the call, but it had to be done.

I explained the situation to both Tom and Jane Ann. I explained that the band was really busy, and that I just couldn't leave in good conscience. So the Nite Raiders would stay together for the winter for sure.

Tom wanted to know what he should do with the MG. Admittedly I hadn't given that a lot of thought, but I understood that Tom and Jane Ann didn't need the extra responsibility of taking care of my car, if I wasn't going to be there until sometime in early January 1970.

I talked to my dad about the car situation. Getting it back to Illinois was not an option. It was serving my needs in Eugene all right, but I wouldn't be back out there for several months, and so I was paying the insurance premium for it to just sit on the street. It seemed logical to have Tom advertise it, and sell it. My dad and I decided that whatever Tom got for the car, probably seven or eight hundred dollars, I would split it with Tom and Jane Ann for their trouble and I would worry about a different car when I got back. Or possibly I would buy a car in Illinois and drive it back to Eugene. At least that problem was solved for the time being.

It was great having Kenny back home and playing music again. The band was starting to expand our reach a little bit more all the time as well. We were playing some gigs in Indiana, but mostly in Illinois.

Olney, Effingham, Robinson, Mattoon, Villa Grove, and of course Newton were regular stops for the band. Fortunately we were busy and making pretty good money for that time. Plus we all had full time jobs, so we were setting pretty well financially. So good in fact that three of the band members had really nice cars.

I remember the day that Kenny and Mike pulled in the exit at the Fairview Drive-In with Kenny's Bronze, 1968 Corvette. I was painting a fence on the other side of the playground when I heard someone pulling in. I turned around to see that beautiful bronze convertible slowly coming in. I couldn't believe my eyes. Of course, if anyone ever deserved to have a Corvette, Kenny certainly did.

Not too long after Kenny got his Corvette, Greg Crouse came driving into band practice in a silver 1968 Corvette convertible. It was immaculate, and believe me Greg wouldn't have it any other way. Even though Greg's left leg was badly hurt and stiff from his accident, he could still get in and out of the Corvette. Greg had one of the strongest wills of anyone I have ever known.

Jeff Dalton drove a very clean and sharp 1964 Pontiac Tempest Le Mans. It was a burgundy two door hard top with a 326 V8; and I believe he had the 4-speed as well. It had enough power that, from time to time, he would pull a small U-Haul trailer behind it for at least part of our band equipment, depending how far we had to travel.

I had at my disposal either my parents Oldsmobile or a '59 Ford station wagon. I know as my old friend Blair would say—"COMPLAINTS at least you got wheels," but something was wrong with this picture. It was time for me to start looking for my own wheels again.

After my hitting the proverbial behavioral wall, and realizing that I had to be more in control of my life, my relationship with my parents and especially my dad, began to improve. My work habits improved as well. My dad didn't have to worry about me showing up for work on time, or getting the show put together for the next day. Admittedly I felt better about myself too. I still went out to have beverages and have fun with my friends, but I tried very hard to keep in mind that there had to be an "on and off switch" to drinking and other activities.

The drive-in season had been very good and quite busy. But the fact was it was starting to wind down. By late August, school was back in session, and even though we would be open on week-ends into October, the fact was that eventually, other than the band income, I would need to have a steady paycheck. I certainly would need the income if I was going to be buying another car. I really wanted to have my own wheels again, but on the other hand the thought of driving all the way back to Eugene in the winter was not all that appealing either.

For the time being though, keeping the band working regularly and tweaking the act to maintain our reputation as a tight professional band was number one on the list. Every member of the band was on board with that.

Part Twenty Four

Out of the Clouds

Sometime in late September or early October 1969, Don Hayes, Blair's stepfather, was paroled out of Menard Correctional Center. I was unaware that he was out of prison until I got a call one afternoon. Don asked me if I would take him to Effingham—the supposed reason—I can't remember. I didn't quite know what to do. I certainly still cared for Jan (Blair's mom). Why she couldn't take him, I can only assume was, that she didn't want to be around him if he was going to do something that would violate his parole. So I told him that I would take him. I was uncomfortable about it, but I had been so close to Blair that I guess I was somehow feeling like it would be one last favor for Blair and Jan.

I knew his reputation. I knew that he was a con man, and had a way of getting in people's pockets and passing bad checks, and he was an alcoholic. But I also thought that he would play it straight with me, especially since I brought Jan down to see him right after Blair's death. I also knew that if I was going to haul him around, I didn't want to do it by myself. I called Mike Yager to see if he was available for the evening. Fortunately he was, and I picked him up on the way into town.

I picked Don up at Jan's trailer. As we headed to Effingham, I asked him what he needed to do there. He said he was going to meet some old friends and maybe play some cards. Other than that it was general small talk, some of it about Blair and none of it about prison. When we got to Effingham Don directed me to where he wanted to go to meet his friends. It was downtown on south Banker Street. He had me stop in front of an old bar called The Oasis. As he was getting out of the car, I asked when we should be back to pick him up. He said "oh maybe a couple hours. You guys come back about 9:00 o'clock ok? See you later." With that he slammed the door and headed in to the bar.

I thought; oh this is great. I just dropped off a parolee and known alcoholic at a bar for two hours, what could possibly go wrong. Mike and I drove around Effingham, doing the normal cruise route in my parents' nice white Oldsmobile sedan—what a chick magnet it was. Somehow we managed to kill a couple hours, and at about 9:00 I drove back down to the Oasis to get Don. Obviously he was not standing out front waiting on us. I really didn't know what to expect, as far as what condition he might be in. I told Mike that I would go in and retrieve him, and hopefully we could get this situation behind us.

When I went into the old bar it was packed and hazy with smoke. I looked quickly at the seats at the bar, hoping I would spot Don. Now all the older guys in the bar were looking at me, I'm sure wondering who this young punk was that showed up in their old hangout. I walked on in and as I looked toward the back where there were some tables, I spotted Don. He was playing poker with four or five other guys. I went to the table, and noticed that he had an almost full cocktail in front of him, as well as a few bills scattered about.

When he saw me, he just said to his fellow players "hey this is my ride here. This is Ron my son's friend, he brought me over here." One guy actually looked up and grunted some sort of a greeting, but no one else even acknowledged that I was there. I said "well Don…are you ready to go?" I already had a bad feeling about what his response was going to be, and he verified it with his response. He said "no-no I'm not ready to go. I've got a drink here and we're talking and playing cards…we're just getting the game going good here." "Tell you what…you and your buddy come back in a couple hours and get me I'll be ready to go then."

I instinctively said "two hours…come on Don I can't…." then I stopped because now all the old guys at the table are looking at me like—hey kid beat it. I also felt like everyone else in the smoky joint was staring and thinking the same thing. So I said "ok two hours" and walked out of the place. I was very unhappy, and mad at myself for getting both Mike and me in to this situation, but as the old saying goes—no good deed goes unpunished.

I told Mike what the situation was. We cussed and discussed what to do for the next two hours. I thought that if Don was mildly defiant at 9:00 o'clock after two hours of drinking, what will he be like at 11:00 after four hours of drinking. I frankly don't remember what Mike and I did to kill another two hours, but I know it was an uneasy two hours.

As we turned back down south Banker toward the Oasis, I have to admit I felt a little anxious and a little angry at the same time. I had enough experience around bars to know that it would be smokier and drunker in the old bar at 11:00 than it was two hours ago. I had already decided that if Don refused to come with me this time, then he was on his own. I'd spent enough time giving him his chance to get drunk and play poker.

Fortunately the card game had broken up and Don was sitting at the bar. He was totally wasted. However, he didn't argue about leaving. He simply chugged his cocktail and said very sloppily "ok Ronnie I'm ready" and climbed off the bar stool and staggered toward the door. I don't remember why, but when we got to the car, Don ended up sitting in the front seat between Mike and me.

As we were leaving Effingham, Don says "hey I'm not going to Newton." Shocked with that news, I said "not going to Newton...then where are you going?" He says "Olney...I need to go to Olney." Neither Mike nor I said anything for a little while, but I was thinking—what in the hell did I get myself and my good friend Mike into here.

I turned south in Dieterich and headed down the Clay City black top. It was the quickest way I knew to get to Olney and deposit our drunken parolee. About two miles south of Dietrich, Don thankfully passed out. He slumped down in the seat between Mike and me. I cranked the big Oldsmobile up well over the speed limit and made a mad dash for Olney. I had to get this situation over with.

About the time we got to Clay City, Mike says "so where are you taking him in Olney?" I said "well there's only one place I know to take him and that's his mother-in-law's house." Mike says "are you sure that's where he wants to go?" I said "that's the only place I know to take him so that's where he's going." I had been to Jan's mother's house once before to meet her mother and her sisters after Blair had died. In the meantime, Don was still totally zonked. He wasn't saying a word.

When we pulled in on the west side of Olney, I had to look carefully to be sure I pulled in to the correct driveway. There were no lights on in his mother-in-law's house, and I assumed that both Mike and I would need to help him in the house. As I pulled in the driveway I started trying to get Don awake. I poked him with my elbow a little and said "Don we're here...we're at your mother-in law's place." Don roused a little bit and said very sleepily and sloppily "where are we?" and I said "we're in Olney at your mother-in law's place isn't that where you wanted to go?" Don shot upright in the seat shouting "NO...NO not my mother-in-law's!!" At the same time he sat upright, he jammed his left foot and leg across the console and directly on to the gas pedal. The Oldsmobile responded quickly and lurched forward, spinning the back tires. I had not had time to put the car in park when I pulled in. I jammed my foot on the brakes as hard as I could, all the while yelling at Don to get his foot off the gas pedal.

I started banging on his leg and pulling it back as I tried to get the car to stop. Finally he realized what was going on and took his foot and leg back across the console. I finally got the car in park. Don was still yelling "NO...NO not here- get the hell out of here, this is not where I want to go!!" Mike and I were both trying to calm him down, as he was now using his arms and hands to get his point across.

As I quickly backed out of the driveway I said, "so where the hell do you want to go?" Don was awake now and agitated about the fact that I had taken him to the only place I knew to go with him. He said "downtown... I'll tell you how to get there." As I drove to downtown Olney, Don had me turn south on Whittle Ave. There was a bar right before the railroad tracks, on the west side of the street. He said "here...right here you can drop me off." I pulled in front of the place, and Mike got out so Don could get out. I said "so how will you get home?" Don said "hey don't worry about it, I have friends here. Thanks a lot." He went in the old bar, and I was truly hoping that was the last I would see or hear from Don Hayes. I would be wrong.

I didn't sleep well at all that night. I couldn't stop thinking about the whole situation. I had apologized to Mike for getting him in the mess, but I still felt really bad about it. I also thought about the fact that Blair never had a good father-son relationship in his short life. That's probably why he liked being around our house so much. And Jan, putting up with an alcoholic con man and thief; I know that she tried hard to make something good out of it, but it just wasn't to be.

The next morning as we all assembled for some breakfast, I told my parents what had taken place the night before. They were both glad that we made it home safely, and like me hoped that would be the last time I had to deal with Don.

About ten o'clock that morning our phone rang. I answered it. It was Don. He wanted to know if I could come to Olney, and bring him back to Newton. I couldn't believe he had the nerve to call me again so soon. I told him to hang on, and I told my dad what was going on. My dad got a very serious look on his face and said "tell him you'll come and get him, but I'm going with you." I told Don that I would be down and asked him where he was. Not surprisingly he was in a bar. Not the same one I had dropped him at, another one on Main Street.

There wasn't a lot of conversation on the way down to Olney. I think my dad knew that I was already very upset about the situation. I had told him that I felt that it was one last favor to do for Blair and for Jan. He understood that, but he too was very upset about it.

When we got to Olney and found the bar downtown, I went in by myself to get Don. Fortunately he hadn't been there long enough to be drunk, and thankfully he wasn't hesitant to go with me. When we got to the car, my dad got out to let Don sit in the front seat. Don told my dad that he was glad to meet him and extended his hand. My dad was a gentleman, and even though he was quite disgusted, he shook Don's hand and got in the back seat.

Most of the conversation on the way back was Don telling my dad how much he appreciated me coming to get him, and how much he appreciated me taking him to Effingham. My dad was mostly unresponsive to it all, just an "uh-huh" once in a while. Surprisingly Don wanted to go to Jan's house. I pulled in the drive and put the car in park. Don looked at me and said "Mr. Kinder you've got a fine boy there" and got out of the car. My dad got out of the back seat, closed the door and walked up in front of Don. My dad said "I know I've got a fine boy there. And mister don't you ever call him again. Do you understand me?" Don simply said "yes sir I understand you" and he turned and went up the stairs.

There wasn't a lot of conversation on the way home. There really didn't need to be. My dad had put an end to it with just a few words. That was the last I heard from Don Hayes.

Fall rolled on and the crisp, cool days were a reminder that winter was closing in. Even though the Nite Raiders were busy, as far as a week-end band goes, I had to come to the realization that if I was staying for the winter, and I was going to buy another car, I had to have a full time job as well.

Kenny was already working at Holt's Lumber Co. He was working down the hill from the lumber yard in what was simply known as the rafter shop. Ironically the land that the rafter shop and rafter storage sat on was part of the lot where my grandpa and grandma Kinder had lived when Roger, Jerry and I used to ride the little red wagon down the hill. That seemed so long ago.

Holt's made rafters for pole barns, which they built in a large area, and also made custom rafters for houses in the shop. It was a booming business, and the number of rafters produced was pretty amazing for a privately owned, family business, in a little town like Newton.

It helped of course that I knew Kenny, and I also knew Vic Ward, who worked in the office at Holt's, plus I knew Donnie Smith who happened to be a huge fan of the Nite Raiders. That all helped when I put my application in to work in the rafter shop. Luckily I got an interview with Mr. Holt (Jesse) right away. I seem to remember that both Vic and Donnie came in during the introduction phase of it, and said some kind words about me and mentioned that I had a good work ethic. Then Mr. Holt called Lee Holt in to meet me, and I suppose give his ok to me being hired for the rafter shop. Lee was the foreman for the rafter shop and Lyle Holt was the foreman for the pole barn crews. Anyway, it worked out well for me and I was hired for the rafter shop, and I believe I probably started in early November.

Now my search for a car could get more serious. With two of my band mates already driving a Corvette, I have to admit that I was leaning strongly in that direction. Admittedly I was thinking about how cool it would be if three out of the four band members had a Corvette, but realistically, I didn't know if it was even possible to find one that I could afford, and then there were the insurance payments as well. But I was young and confident that with a full time job and the band income, I could probably pull it off, so I began to watch the ads in the local paper, as well as the Decatur paper. The serious search was on.

When I mentioned to my dad that I had decided to look for a Corvette, he was less than thrilled with me. Unlike the other cars that I had paid for, he told me that he would have nothing to do with me buying a Corvette. What he meant was; he wouldn't go to the bank with me to give his blessing, if Mr. Pickerel agreed to loan the money. So I was on my own if I found a 'Vette to buy. I never really knew why he was so opposed to me buying a Corvette, but he had let me know what he thought, and that was that.

I actually had a pretty good relationship with Mr. Pickerel at the People's State Bank, and I was now twenty one and gainfully employed, so I felt good about being able to talk to him on my own if the opportunity presented itself. I had paid off three other notes for cars, and felt pretty confident that I could do it again.

Top left: Roger Kinder, 1964 Dodge Dart

Top right: Roger Kinder, 1969 Plymouth GTX

Center: Ron & Kenny's 1963 Chevy Super Sport

Bottom left: Ron's 1964 MG 1100

Bottom Right: Ron & Janice with his 1967 Corvette

Part Twenty Five

Almost Perfect Weather

Sometime in the third week of November, I saw an ad in the Decatur paper for a 1967 Corvette. After a brief description, it had an additional little statement on the bottom. "Must Sell." It was as though the ad was targeting me. It was as though they knew I would see it. Ok maybe that's a bit of an exaggeration, but it definitely got my attention. The ad said the Corvette had a 327-4 speed, and it was a convertible. I couldn't get to the phone fast enough.

The owner's wife answered the phone, and I told her I was calling about the Corvette. She told me that he was at work and wouldn't be home until after 5:00. Anyway, after a couple more phone calls, I was able to set up an appointment with the guy to see the car. Mike Yager was able to go with me to Mt. Zion to see the car. The owner was a partner in a drag racing team called "The Wild Child" and because they were in the process of buying a new car and other equipment, to make the team even more professional, the guys wife had told him that if he was going to spend that kind of money on the race team, then the Corvette had to go.

In fact, he had already sold the actual convertible top from the car for extra cash, leaving the car with a hard top only. However, it didn't mean that I wasn't interested because of that. The Corvette was Marlboro Maroon with saddle interior. It did indeed have a 327 with a 4 speed. That was exactly what I wanted. I didn't actually want a 427 at the time, due to the insurance cost for young people. The tires were "red line" and in great shape.

If I had been like a kid in a candy store when I looked at the '63 Chevy Super Sport, then I was a kid in a candy store and I was drooling while looking at this car. We dickered back and forth for a few minutes; the seller pointing to the low miles and condition of the car in general, and I used the fact that it had no convertible top and that hurt the value. We finally agreed on $3250.00. The car had sold originally for around $4250.00, so his asking price was reasonable for the time. The sale was contingent on me securing the loan from Mr. Pickerel at the Peoples State Bank.

As soon as possible I went to the bank and asked to see Mr. Pickerel. There may have been others at the bank to talk to about loans, but I had only dealt with Mr. Pickerel, and he had always been fair and respectful. When Mr. Pickerel told me to come in, I have to admit to being a little nervous. If he had asked me what my dad thought about me buying a Corvette, it could have meant the deal was not happening.

Fortunately when I told him that I wanted to buy a Corvette, he actually smiled, and said "oh a Corvette huh, well what year?" As I described the car to him, I'm sure he could sense my excitement and enthusiasm about it. Next he wanted to know how much I wanted to borrow. I had a few bucks in my savings account, but not much. I told Mr. Pickerel that I needed to borrow $3000.00.

Frankly I hadn't even thought about the fact that I had no collateral to offer for such a loan. I suppose because my dad had done so much business with him—all the drive in business went through the People's State Bank—and the fact that I had paid off three cars previously, he didn't even ask what collateral I had to offer. He said "ok we'll loan you the money on one condition, as soon as you get it, I want to see it." Man I was so happy to hear those words, I was a little flustered. I said "oh sure—absolutely I'll bring it by to show you—thank you—thank you very much."

What had just happened was amazing. Mr. Pickerel, on my word, and my dad's reputation, had just given me an unsecured loan on a car that he had never seen. As excited as I was, it took a little while for that to sink in. I called the seller in Mt. Zion as soon as I got home, and told him that I got the money. He was happy, I was happy, and we made arrangements for me to come to Mt. Zion and close the deal on the Saturday after Thanksgiving, November 29th. Man what a great Thanksgiving this was going to be.

I called Yager's house as soon as I made arrangements with the seller. I needed someone to take me to Mt. Zion, so I could drive my new car home. As it turned out Mike was the one who could go on that Saturday as well, I'm not sure what Kenny was doing. So it was set. Mike would drive me up there to get the deal done, and I could bring the beautiful '67 Corvette home.

Thanksgiving Day, November 27, 1969 was a typical late November day in Illinois. It was cloudy and cold, and rather dreary looking. My parents had invited Jan Hayes to come out and have the traditional Thanksgiving meal with us. She didn't really have anywhere else to go. After the delicious meal that my mom prepared and a lot of conversation on various subjects, I became rather bored and asked to be excused, and borrowed the parents' Oldsmobile to head into town and see what was shaking in there.

The main "drag" route in Newton was usually a trip or two around the square, turn south on Van Buren St. and make your way slowly down to the turnaround at Neese's gas station. Turn back north toward the square and typically go to the corner of Jourdan and Van Buren and turn right toward the Dog 'n Suds. Make your way past the bowling alley, past Dulgar's Seed House and make a circle around the Dog 'n Suds, checking out who was there. If you didn't stop to visit or get a coney dog and root beer, you went back to the highway, turned right and "got on it" for at least one shift, maybe two, depending on what you were driving.

Many people after a couple trips around the "drag" would either stop in Dulgar's parking lot to watch and see who all was in town, or you could assemble at Dick Wagner's house—between the bowling alley and Dulgar's—and hang out on the front porch—with other classmates, friends, and "outlaws" and watch the traffic from there. I must say something about Dick's mom Pat Wagner. She was one of those ladies that could put up with all the friends and classmates dropping by at all times of the day and night. But she expected people to show some respect and not destroy the place, no matter how much fun you may be having. One of my memories of Pat has stuck with me for all these years. It usually came if either Dick or someone else would ask Pat to get them a beer or a soda or a sandwich etc. instead of just going to get it themselves. Pat would simply say—so everyone could hear it—"what's wrong with you, you got an anchor in your ass?" It was funny every time I heard it, and I think people used to do it just to be able to hear Pat say that. She certainly put up with a lot from all of us. I hope she knew how much we really liked her for it.

So it was on that Thanksgiving Day, I had made a couple of trips around the square, and took the abbreviated trip down to Dick's house, to just hang out and get all the latest gossip. Several people were already there, and I joined them on the front porch. After a few minutes a car pulled in the yard, right up by the porch. It was my friend "Sam", a girl from our high school class, and another girl. I thought I should know her, but I just wasn't sure. She rolled down the window and said "hello." The conversation generally was between "Sam" and Dick. I have no idea what they were saying, because I couldn't take my eyes off the girl with the coal black hair, snapping brown eyes, and a beautiful smile.

The conversation ended, and "Sam" pulled out of the yard and back on the highway. I immediately said "who was that girl?" Dick says "that's Janice Moran, you know, she used to be (a former classmate's) girl." I said "so that's Janice Moran huh-wow I didn't realize she was that good looking. Wait you said "she used to be his girl?" "They broke up?" Dick says "yep-they broke up."

I said "ok well I believe I'll take a little drive around town then. See you guys later." I got in the big white Oldsmobile and headed for the square. I thought of a quick plan to see if I could somehow end up with the girl that I'd never met, but certainly wanted to. As I went around the square and turned east on Washington Street, sure enough here came "Sam" with the two young ladies, heading west. We both stopped, rolled the windows down, and I quickly said "hey why don't you guys get in a ride around with me?" As expected "Sam" says "well that would be stupid, why don't you just park that thing and get in with us you dumbass?" Bingo!! The quick plan had worked just as I planned it. And as it turned out, since they were all in the front seat of "Sam's" car, someone needed to get in the back seat with me…and what do you know, the person that moved to the back was…Janice Moran. My little plan had worked, and little did I know then, but that little plan would change my life forever.

Though the conversation may have been a little clumsy, due to the fact that we had never met or been introduced before, we managed to at least get acquainted as we rode around town. Slowly I started to relax a little because she was actually easy to talk to. I eventually worked up the courage to ask her if she would like to go to the Crystal Club that evening, to listen to some music. To my surprise, she said that she would go. I couldn't believe it. I was trying not to act like a little boy that just opened a birthday gift, and found a new baseball glove, but it was hard not to.

"Sam" and my classmate also decided that they would go to the Crystal as well. We made plans to meet later that evening and it would be a "double date."

Well as it turned out something went wrong, as far as the other couple meeting us, and I couldn't believe it, but I had Janice all to myself for the evening. I was happy, excited, thrilled, ecstatic, and a little worried. Yeah…a little worried. It had actually been a while since I had had "a first date."

And this date was a first for more than one reason. I had only met Janice Moran a few hours ago, and I found out on the way there, that she had never been to the Crystal before.

But the first date went exceptionally well. After a couple hours the nervousness all went away. We were actually comfortable around each other, and had a great time. Janice told me however, that she needed to be home by midnight to meet with her dad's curfew. I had her back in Newton in time for her to make her curfew, but we made plans for the following night. The Nite Raiders were playing at the Crystal on Friday and Saturday night, plus I told her about the fact that I had to go to Mt. Zion on Saturday morning to pick up the Corvette. How much more could you pack in to a weekend? We were about to find out.

Part Twenty Six

Not a Cloud in the Sky

That Friday night, November 28, Janice made arrangements to come to the Crystal with her friend and my former classmate. Part of the reason was so that she could go back to her friend's mobile home in Charleston to spend the night, therefore, not having to worry about the midnight curfew at home. The hours for bands at the Crystal were 9:00 to 1:00. That night Janice and I made arrangements for me to come over to Charleston, after I had made the deal for the Corvette, and pick her up. Mike Yager and Janice were actually classmates, so he followed me over to Charleston and we all chatted for a while. I wasn't really there to talk. I was only interested in picking up Janice and getting the heck out of there.

So the first official passenger in my "new" Corvette was Janice Moran. As we drove south on Route 130 towards Newton, I wished that the trip was going to be longer. I mean, come on, I had a long black haired beauty sitting in the passenger seat of my "new" '67 Corvette, and she seemed to like me well enough to want to actually be with me three times in the same weekend, what's not to go crazy for?

But I had promised Mr. Pickerel that I would bring the new car by as soon as the deal was done, so I had to get there as soon as I dropped Janice off at home. However, we made plans for me to come back and pick her up later, and she would go to hear the Nite Raiders play again. My head was spinning. I couldn't even believe what all had happened this weekend, and it wasn't over yet.

I parked the Corvette in front of the bank, so that if Mr. Pickerel looked out the window he would be able to see it easily. I waited until he finished with another customer, and he motioned for me to come in. I actually started the conversation.

I said "well Mr. Pickerel you said as soon as I got the Corvette, that you wanted to see it, so it's sitting out front." You couldn't have wiped the smile off my face with a brush. Mr. Pickerel said "oh it is...well let's see what you got." He got up from his chair and went to the front window, and pulled back the drapes. He looked for a few seconds and said "well...yes that's very nice, very pretty car. You should be proud of it." I said "oh I am very proud of it." Then Mr. Pickerel says "I'll give you six months." I took a big gulp of air and said "six months?" I thought he had changed his mind and was only going to give me six months to pay for the car. He said "yeah…six months and you'll be married." Now I could breathe again. I laughed and said "married…No I don't think so I'm not planning on that any time soon." Mr. Pickerel never changed the expression on his face and said again "I'll give you six months. Yes that's a nice car Ronnie, take good care of it and enjoy it."

I thanked him profusely for trusting me, and for giving me the loan, and we said our good byes. My head was still spinning from all that had taken place so far on this Thanksgiving weekend. As I got back in my car I thought about what Mr. Pickerel had said, he'd give me six months. I had to chuckle; that was not going to happen. I was thinking more like…let the good times roll.

On Saturday evening I went down to pick Janice up for our "date." It was not a normal date really, since I was actually going to play, and then tear down equipment, but at least she would be there to talk to during the breaks. On top of all the things that had happened so far, I got to meet Janice's family. I met her dad George, mother Ada Mae, and her little sister Mary Jo, and little brother Joe. Everything went very smoothly, but before Janice and I could get out the door her dad, with sort of a smile on his face, says "well...I guess you won't have this girl home by midnight then?" Man I was hoping that subject wouldn't come up, but I gave it my best shot. I didn't really have a smile, it was more of a panicked look, and I said "well...no...actually the band plays until 1:00...so no I guess not." George said to both of us "well get home as soon as you can then, and be careful." And then more to Janice, but at least with a smile he said "if you get in some kind of trouble you can't get out of—call me."

So that was the first meeting. I definitely understood that I did not score any bonus points for being the reason that Janice wouldn't be home by midnight, but I thought it would certainly be worth it. I could handle Mr. Moran being upset with me, as long as he didn't refuse to let his daughter go out with me.

With all the excitement of the phenomenal Thanksgiving weekend, it was probably sometime in the first week of December that reality finally sat in. My plans were supposed to be that come January first I needed to be headed back to Eugene and start school about the middle of January. All of a sudden I had a lot to think about. With all that had happened recently, Eugene seemed 10,000 miles away.

First of all, I couldn't stop thinking about Janice. It had been a total accident that we met at all, and now I didn't want twenty-four hours to go by and not at least talk to her. Secondly, I was so excited that I found the Corvette, and it was exactly what I had expected it would be. Admittedly I had not given a lot of thought to the fact that, if I indeed went back to Eugene, I would be driving across both the Rocky Mountains and the Cascade Mountains to get there.

Third, the band was very busy, playing most every Friday and Saturday night. Plus we were able to ask for and usually get more money than we ever had before. I know all the members felt that we were as tight and solid as we had ever been.

I knew that more than likely I had a job waiting for me at the Bon Marche. I really had been excited about going to Lane Community College and studying drama. I had made some great new friends there, and Tom and Jane Ann had opened there home to me and accepted me as a member of the family. I couldn't be more grateful for that.

I had more thoughts going through my head all at the same time than I had ever had before. I had the car that I had been talking about since I had first seen Frank Yager's 1960 Corvette, black with a silver insert. Or Tony Arndt's beautiful red 1964 roadster that every high school kid my age was so jealous of. But, my Corvette was in reality, just a car. If I had to, I could painfully give up the car.

The band was also something to be proud of. We had worked hard every week since we got back together to get better, and we had done that. But if necessary, to make a better life for myself, I could give up the band.

But what I was not willing to do, was go back to Eugene, Oregon and leave Janice Moran in Jasper County. That was more than my brain would accept. We had only known each other for a few days, and I hadn't even mentioned to Janice that I was considering going back to Eugene. But something different was going on here. This had a different feel. As chaotic and rowdy and sometimes out of control as my life had been over the past several months, I felt something I hadn't felt for quite some time. I felt at peace.

I felt that things were going to be alright. I felt that I had made the right decision to stay in Jasper County and start my life over. I felt that just maybe all the searching, and all the dead end roads that I had been on, were finally making the right turn after all. I couldn't wait to find out.

Part Twenty Seven

Cold Days and Warm Nights

On December 11, 1969 my cousin Roger was discharged from the Marine Corps. It had been exactly one year ago that he left Viet Nam. Almost three years since he and Eddie Groves left together for basic training. In June of 1969 Roger had gotten married and was now waiting on a new arrival in the family. It was all part of the transition from military life back to civilian life that hundreds of thousands of young men were making during the Viet Nam era.

There were still over 300,000 U.S. troops on the ground in Viet Nam at the beginning of 1970[26]. My lifetime friend Bruce Ward was still there, and would be for over three more months. Spec. 6 Anthony "Tony" Housh was still listed as missing in action. So as good as my life was going at the end of 1969, many of our friends and family and acquaintances were still dealing with an enemy that many times they couldn't see, sleeping in the mud, with the snakes, biting bugs and the heat in the Viet Nam jungle. Many were now fighting there battles and demons at home. Some would overcome them, but many could not.

Kenny Yager was probably doing the best job of getting back to a normal life that I had seen. If anyone would have had the right to be a little out of control or push the envelope it would have been Kenny. He had seen and been through a lot, both before and after he was wounded. Fortunately he was back playing music, he had been able to buy a great looking Corvette, and he now had a steady girlfriend. Life was actually pretty good for "young Kenneth" as well.

Kenny and I were both driving our Corvette's to work at Holt's Lumber Co. I still had trouble believing that we had those cars, and that we were working in the same place. I also couldn't believe that on some occasions when the Nite Raiders were playing at the Crystal Club, there would be three 'vettes backed up to the stage door. It was a very cool situation. It was not that we were bragging about it, it was more of a "can you frickin' believe how far we've come since we were playing for $50 bucks and all the fish you can eat" kind of thing. It had been quite a transition for the Nite Raiders as well.

Kenny began coming in to work looking like he had forgotten to get some sleep the night before. It was happening more and more, and the other guys at the rafter shop, and certainly me, started razzing him about it. It was pretty obvious that Kenny was concentrating on something besides sleep. He took a lot of good natured ribbing over it, but fortunately he was always a good sport about it, and generally just laughed it off.

And then sometime in mid-December 1969, Kenny told me that the—maybe not so unexpected—had happened, and he was going to be a father. Now it was a little more serious conversation. Now plans for a wedding were being made, and where were they going to live and all those things that come into the reality of it all. Transition comes unexpectedly sometimes. So now, two of my closest friends were going to be fathers. Both had been to war, both had made it back to Jasper County, and man how things had changed since that summer of 1966.

The Nite Raiders played the New Year's Eve gig (Wednesday the 31st) at the Crystal Club that year. We knew there would be a full house. We normally drew a good crowd anyway, and typically more people took advantage of the chance to really "whoop it up" and act foolish on New Year's

Eve. And sure enough they did not disappoint on this particular night. We started at 9:00 and the place was already a "zoo" by that time. Apparently a lot of people had started the celebration early in the afternoon.

About 9:30, right out in front of me, a whale of a fight started. Tables were turned over, glasses were crashing, and fists were flying. People were scattering out of the way. Those involved in the fight were yelling and cussing. The bouncers were trying to get everyone separated, but it was hard to get in and find out who all was involved. When the "dust" cleared and I got a good look at the chaos, I saw a rather large woman sitting on top of a guy, who was on his back on the floor, and she was pounding away on the guy's head. The bouncers finally got to her and pulled her off of the guy, who was now quite bloody. It was a total mess and it took a few minutes to get the tables back in place and chairs sat back up, and for people to quiet down. It took the bouncers a few minutes to get the brawlers out the front door too. Some of them at least, were not willing to go peacefully.

But during all the fighting and yelling and general confusion; the band never missed a beat. We kept playing like nothing strange was going on at all. That wasn't the first bar fight that we'd played through. We actually got a good laugh out of that one, especially when we saw the woman beating the snot out of the poor guy on the floor.

We played that night and the following night, Thursday January 1, 1970. The next night was a lot calmer. A good crowd, but not the necessarily the early day drinkers, like the night before. Janice didn't go with me for those two gigs. I had actually told her that those two nights, it might be best for her to just stay home and be safe. And as it turned out, I was right.

On December 19, 1969 Kenny was married. That in itself was hard to comprehend. I had just never pictured Kenny as being married, let alone being a father. It seemed like just a few months ago we were trying to figure out which keg party to go to, and driving around in our old Pontiacs. It was like "hey hold on here—slow down—this can't be happening." But it was happening, and that wasn't all.

Sometime later in January, on a Friday, Lee Holt came down to the rafter shop with the paychecks, which was always a good thing to see. Normally Lee would try to "yuck it up" with the guys in the shop, but this Friday he was acting a little bit more serious. Eventually he got around to the business at hand. He explained to us that business was slowing down for now and the foreseeable future, and that he was going to have to lay us all off.

An awkward silence drifted through the shop. Lee was uncomfortable with the silence as well and quickly said "well it's just temporary…I mean we want you back…we're not firing you…it's just until business picks up again." I got a nasty feeling in my gut of course, but as bad as I felt for myself, I felt even worse for Kenny. He had been married probably all of a month, and now he's laid off for…well we didn't know how long.

I'm not sure about Kenny or the other guys in the shop, but I had never been laid off from a job before. I had quit and moved on, but never had been told I was laid off. I wasn't sure what we were supposed to do. I didn't know the first thing about drawing unemployment, or how you even went about it, but Kenny and I were about to go find out; like it or not.

I believe that the first trip to the unemployment office in Effingham, we went together. I remember that I at least, was like a new kid in school. I didn't know you had to answer so many questions or that you had to tell them how much experience you had and how much you made at the different jobs.

When we left I felt as though I had forgotten to study for a test, and probably flunked it.

I guess after it was all sorted out, I ended up with about two thirds of what I was making at Holt's. Thankfully the band stayed busy, and I was able to get by, at least for a while. The humorous part of the whole thing, to me at least, was that Kenny and I were, I'm sure, the only two guys driving a Corvette to the unemployment office on a weekly basis. It didn't take long to get tired of the whole situation of dealing with the unemployment office. I believe it took three weeks to get the first check, and it didn't seem like it was worth the hassle, especially with all the driving back and forth.

One thing that was certainly worth the effort was the fact that I was still dating Janice. Even though she was working full time at Norris Electric, we could still go out for short dates in the evening or I would just go down and hang out with the family and watch TV. I didn't care as long as I was getting to see Janice, plus I knew I had to make some points back with her dad for totally obliterating the midnight curfew rule he had. Fortunately for me, Janice seemed to enjoy going with me to the Nite Raiders gigs. She said that she enjoyed watching me play. But I don't think that her dad ever accepted the fact that bands playing in bars or clubs didn’t even stop playing until 12:00 midnight, or many times 1:00 am.

Part Twenty Eight

Clear Skies Ahead

My parents and my Aunt Fern couldn't hide their joy that I had found someone that seemed to be able to change my attitude and my habits all at the same time. It's not that I had stopped drinking, but now I had a lot to think about besides going out to party. In fact, it seemed that I had somehow chosen to date the only girl in Ste. Marie that didn't drink beer. We had a lot of laughs about that. In fact I don't think Janice even cared if she had a drink at all. She generally had something just to be sociable. I told her she was certainly a cheap date. We had some laughs about that too.

I never lost focus about the band however. We were a tight unit, and we all had respect for the other members. And it just happened to be the only income that Kenny and I had for the time being. I knew then, and certainly have thought about it for many years, just how fortunate we were to have the talent of Jeff Dalton in our band. We were all pretty darn good at what we did, but with Jeff handling keyboards, saxophone, and vocals plus he was just enough older than the rest of us that he had a leadership quality that really helped.

Luckily we stayed busy for the winter and into March, but the band income couldn't sustain me forever. Even though I was living at home, the insurance on the Corvette was much higher than cars I'd had before, plus I needed to be socking away some savings in case something unexpected came along.

On Friday, March 13, 1970 I went down and picked Janice up, and we came back to the Fairview Drive-In. It was an unusual off night for the band, and the drive-in was just beginning to be open on weekends. My parents needed the income as well. We watched a little of the movie that was on, and I nervously excused myself, telling Janice that I needed to get something out of the car. When I returned, I was even more nervous. The reason for my nervousness was that I went to retrieve what I hoped would be an engagement ring that I had purchased at Rauch's Jewelry. My finances being what they were at the time, I had told Mr. Rauch that I needed to stay at about a hundred dollars. He said "oh...a hundred dollars...well let's see what we can find." I knew I was being a cheapskate but I had to be realistic about how much money I had. Luckily we found something that was "pretty nice" and the engagement ring and wedding band combination was $94.00 plus tax. It had a little sparkle of a diamond on it, and I told him that it was perfect.

When I went back in the house, Janice had moved over to my dad's favorite chair and was reading the paper. I went behind her, put my arms and hands around her shoulders--keeping the ring box hidden—and made one of the oddest proposals that had probably ever been made. I said "Janice if I can find a job, will you marry me?" And with that I opened the box to expose the ring. I guess when two people are in love, it wouldn't matter if it was a toy out of a Cracker Jack's box. Janice stood up and with a beautiful smile said "yes."

Friday the 13th was actually a very lucky day for me. It was one of the happiest days of my life. I'm not sure what I would have done if she would have said no, because I knew after only meeting her on Thanksgiving Day that I had to be with her from now on.

We walked over to the concession stand to tell my parents, although I think they had a pretty good idea that I wasn't going to let Janice slip away. My mom could now officially relax. I was not going back to Eugene, and I had a definite direction in life. My dad usually didn't say too much about matters of the heart, but he too had a huge smile on his face.

The other side of the story was that now we had to let Janice's parents know that there was going to be a wedding. Sometimes a person just has to admit that they were stupid or ignorant of the facts, or just plain forget.

That was the case with yours truly. I was just so excited and absolutely flip dizzy about asking Janice to marry me that I forgot to talk to George Moran about it beforehand. Even on the way back to Ste. Marie that night, Janice started talking about "how will I tell my dad about it." And then it hit me...I hadn't asked him about it and now it was going to be on Janice to tell him. I could only imagine what he might think or say. Here I was playing in a band, hardly ever getting his daughter back home before midnight, I'm driving a Corvette—and I don't even have a full time job!!

I thought "holy crap he's going to tell her she's crazy." I said "hey maybe I should go in and talk to your dad." Janice said "no...no I'll talk to him. I'll just have to catch him at the right time."

I'm thinking "oh my god, the right time" when will that be—when he's sleeping—when he's eating a big piece of pie—or maybe at church—yeah at Mass. He couldn't come totally unglued in the middle of Mass. Again Janice tried to reassure me that she could handle it, just give her a couple days. So I walked Janice to the front door—before midnight—gave her a big kiss, wished her luck and told her I would see her tomorrow night.

I picked Janice up on Saturday evening. We were on our way to a gig somewhere, and I said "so...did you get a chance to talk to your dad?" She said "no not yet, it just hasn't been the right time." On Sunday I picked Janice up so that we could go somewhere to eat—probably the Green Lantern in Effingham. Same basic conversation "no not yet." Finally, on Monday evening, she found her dad at the barn taking care of the cattle and told him. Luckily there was no screaming—no "are you out of your mind." He actually took it pretty well. Apparently he knew my dad pretty well and knew that he was a gentleman and a man of his word. I guess he hoped at least a little of that had rubbed off on his son. Anyway, it was done. Now I could move on to the next important part; I had to find a job.

In mid-April 1970 I answered an ad for a salesman for the Rockford Life Insurance Co. The local office was located in Effingham. I had never sold anything, other than theater tickets, hot dogs, hamburgers etc. and that really isn't selling. The customer already knew what they wanted. But I had known some people who sold insurance, and it looked as though they had a pretty good life. They wore nice clothes, and generally drove nice cars, and it was clean work, so I thought "what the heck" I'll put in my application. I got an interview with the manager of the office in Effingham, his name was Darrel Lake.

I don't remember much about the interview or the questions he asked, but apparently you didn't have to be an experienced salesman, because he told me that he was willing to give me a shot if I could pass the Illinois state insurance exam and get licensed. I was so young and stupid that I hadn't even thought about the fact that I had to get a license from the state. Darrel Lake gave me a hard cover binder that was about four inches thick and weighed about ten pounds, and told me to start studying and he'd let me know the date to go to Springfield to take the test.

It's been a long time, but I seem to remember that I could start working as long as a licensed agent was with me. I must have started out on a draw (advance against sales commission) because I know I was working before I got my license. And with help from Janice and hard studying I actually passed the test the first time.

The job quite simply was selling life insurance door to door. Also we collected premiums from customers on a monthly basis. It was called a "debit route" and the insurance policies we sold were known as "industrial" policies because they were priced so that people who couldn't afford more expensive policies would be able to have some kind of coverage. The difference being that we went by once a month and personally collected the premium.

Needless to say we worked mostly in the "poorer" sections of the county or town. So here I am driving around in a shiny 1967 Corvette asking people who may or may not even be able to afford a car, or a front door to their house for that matter, to buy life insurance or pay their monthly premium. I began to feel very uncomfortable, especially walking in to a home of a single parent, with three or four little kids running around, and my Corvette is parked outside.

But...I had a job to do, and that was to try and sell insurance to the people who could least afford it. But at least if they had a small policy, their family would have something in case they were all of a sudden not there anymore. I actually did believe that what I was doing was a good thing. I started to have some success. When your first sales job is selling door to door, whatever the product might be, you learn to take no's and doors slamming in your face pretty quickly. If you can't take that, and just go on to the next door and start again, then you may not be ready for an actual sales position. I had some very tough days, and even before we got married, Janice got to hear some stories about what salespeople go through.

June 20, 1970 was the date for the wedding. Almost seven months after I had met Janice, we were going to be married. Mr. Pickerel was off by less than a month. His declaration giving me six months had almost been right on the money. The wedding was large. I chose my cousin Roger as my best man and Mike Yager as my groomsman. Many of my classmates and friends were there. The changes and the shear, sometimes cruel realities that we had all faced in the four years since our high school graduation were secondary on this day.

After our honeymoon trip to Kentucky Lake and Lake Barkley, Janice and I started our lives together in Effingham. Our first apartment was half of a big old house on south Fourth Street. It took a few months for me to accept the reality that I didn't have to give her back. I actually got to keep her. The midnight curfew didn't apply. All the searching for happiness and fulfilment was over. A major transition had taken place...and it was good.

Ron & Janice on their wedding day.

Footnotes and Acknowledgements

1- Department of Defense-Manpower Data Center www.AmericanWarLibrary.com
2- The Riverfront Times
3- Source – Jeff Crouse and Jennifer Crouse Yoder
4- D.O.D. www.AmericanWarLibrary.com
5- Source – Brad Ackerman
6- D.O.D. www.AmericanWarLibrary.com
7- Wikipedia – Leonard B. Scott "The Battle of Hill 875 DakTo, Vietnam 1967" War College
8- With permission from Ron "Delwin" Granby
9- www.TaskForceOmego.org Also re: Tony Housh
10- www.qualityinfo.org/Oregonminimumwage-jobfacts
11- www.wikepedia.org/HAIR
12- www.wikepedia.org/WeatherUnderground
13- www.wikepedia.org/1968theVietnamwar
14- Source – Brad Ackerman
15- www.angelfire.com
16- Source – Conversation with Bruce Ward – Vietnam combat veteran
17- www.registerguard.com
18- Google – Weight gallon oil based paint
19- www.wikepedia.org/Lanecommunitycollege
20- D.O.D. www.Americanwarlibrary.com
21- Newton Press-Mentor
22- www.moongiant.com
23- www.nasa.gov
24- www.wikepedia.org/woodstock
25- www.wikepedia.org/woodstock
26- D.O.D. www.Americanwarcollege.com

Afterwords

Writing about things and events that happened fifty years ago or more can certainly be challenging. In many cases however, all it takes is a little coaxing and the feelings and emotions from long ago come streaming back to you like opening a water spigot. Even though the spigot may be rusty and corroded, once opened it flows out with ease.

I hoped when starting this writing that I could bring back the memories and emotions, both good and bad, about life in a small town during a very turbulent and in some cases, destructive time. It was a time of war. A time that for many turned dark and not easily defined. Most families just kept their feelings and their suffering to themselves. Some things were just not talked about openly, even in a small town.

The comical as well as the tragic events in a small town always seem to be more personal. My hope was to bring the era of the mid to late sixties back to life in a way that, not only people of my generation, but many generations, could relate to. Writing about my life, my family, friends and acquaintances, the events and behavior that young people took part in during that era was both fun and a little scary.

For generations, young people have been launched out into the real world with no particular plan or direction. That was certainly a part of my life, and I hoped to be able to describe the feelings and emotions of not only my life, but to emphasize what can happen when people have absolutely no direction.

Certainly some of my friends and close relatives felt that the best thing they could do was to serve their country, and possibly along the way, they would find a direction. Maybe they could learn a skill that they could hang on to once they were home. Maybe they would grow up a little. Maybe they would find something that they had been searching for. Some did, but some went a little further into the darkness.

Although I was not able to serve, and various life issues caused me and many of my friends to continue to drift, without much real purpose, there were flashes of light. My months in Eugene, Oregon woke me to the fact that sometimes change is really good. I actually felt myself changing, and appreciated being back in a better place. Tom and Jane Ann, the kids, Jack and Joan,

Freddie, Barb, all the people associated with the Very Little Theater, and my job at "The Bon" all helped me to see that I didn't need to escape by drinking etc.

It was not my parents fault, or my friends fault, or my bandmates fault that I seemingly slipped off the rails, once I returned to Jasper County. I assume all the blame for that. But, Thanksgiving Day 1969 was indeed a game changer for me. I know it sounds like too much of a cliché, but the lights came on that day. It made me understand that even though you may be wandering around in a dark place, that there is indeed reason for hope, and there is peace out there for you if you just keep searching.

As of this writing, Janice and I have been married for over forty nine years. I have felt for years and years, that had it not been for the fact that I met Janice, and fortunately married her; I may have continued going around in circles on roads with no end. I hope that this writing helps people realize that there is hope. There is light outside the darkness. Don't give up.

As good as life became after June 20, 1970, no one's life is perfect. Newlyweds then, as they do now, find that there are certainly bumps in the road. Janice and I were no different, but we learned to deal with it together. Plus we both had families that were there and willing to help. What you find out of course is that, every generation faces pretty much the same thing.

I guess most men look back at life and think; when did I really become a man? Well in my case it wasn't the first time I got shot at in combat, as some guys have told me. It wasn't when I won a fight against some guy you were sure would beat you to a pulp.

No...I believe that I finally became a man at about 10:30 am on Thursday June 13, 1974. That is when Ryan Nathan Kinder came into the world. He finally gave up and came out to join us, after thirty two hours of labor on Janice's part. After looking down at that little guy that morning, you couldn't help but know that nothing would ever be the same...but life was good. It has been and continues to be good.

My generation and my classmates from high school all started out pretty much the same. We were all searching for everything. Some were lucky enough to find happiness quickly, some searched for many years. But to get to the next phase of our lives, we all had a big transition to make. Most made the transition, and went on with their lives. Some never got the chance.

If you've read this far then I'll assume that you enjoyed this writing. For that I am very grateful. And as always I am very humbled by it. Thank you very much.

Ron and his '63 Chevy Super Sport

Dedication and Thanks

This book is dedicated to the memory of the following very special people in my life:

My parents—Lamar and Ina Mae Kinder

Jane Ann (Ackerman) Hannaman

Thomas G. Ackerman

Monty J. Blair

Jeff Dalton

Greg Crouse

Harry D. "Buddy" Gowin

Special thanks to the following people for their help in gathering information and giving me permission to share their stories and emotions.

First and most importantly, to my wife Janice for again allowing me to spend the hours, weeks and months to write this book. And for her help in editing and planning.

Roger Kinder for again helping with details and information about Viet Nam, and allowing me to include his story in the book.

Kenny Yager for the interview about his experiences in Viet Nam and for being a good sport about other stories from our youth.

Bruce Ward for his help with details about Viet Nam and for allowing me to speak with his mom Marie.

Mike Yager for reminding me of details about our adventures and when Kenny was wounded.

Ed Groves and his wife Kay for sharing some of the information about Eddie's Viet Nam experiences and details about dates of discharge etc.

The entire staff of the Newton Public Library for their help in my research for the book.

And finally to all the family members, classmates, friends, and acquaintances that served their country during the Viet Nam war. And thank you to Ron Granby for allowing me to share his mother's story.

Made in the USA
Monee, IL
09 December 2020